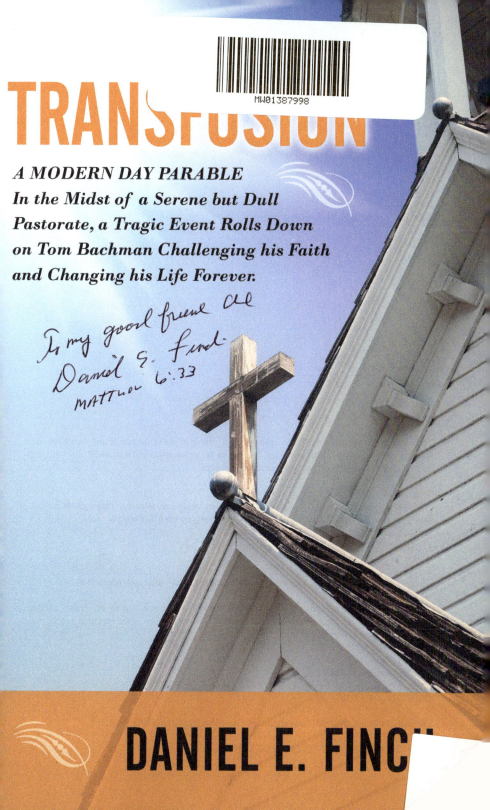

TRANSFUSION

A MODERN DAY PARABLE

In the Midst of a Serene but Dull Pastorate, a Tragic Event Rolls Down on Tom Bachman Challenging his Faith and Changing his Life Forever.

To my good friend Al
Daniel E. Finch
MATThew 6:33

DANIEL E. FINCH

Outskirts Press, Inc.
http://www.outskirtspress.com

ISBN: 978-1-4787-3057-6

Outskirts Press and the "OP" logo are trademarks belonging to Outskirts Press, Inc.

PRINTED IN THE UNITED STATES OF AMERICA

DEDICATION

To Sam and Eva Tadlock
First Converts of the
Rebirth of Sni Mills Church

ENDORSEMENTS

Dr. Dan Finch is a wise pastor and church leader. He truly understands the local church. Dan's passion for people who are far from God is as white-hot today as it was nearly six decades ago when he pastored his first church! In this book, he takes a creative approach of story in novel form and adds practical principles that really work. I have personally seen this model in action and I highly recommend it. --Dan Reiland, Executive Pastor, 12 Stone Church, Author of Amplified Leadership

Dr. Finch has spent his life helping pastors and churches move toward missional obedience. The first part of the book describes a pastor struggling with the routines of stagnant ministry. In the second portion the pastor discovers solutions that are practical, biblical, and easily applied to every local church. It is an exciting read but more so, it is written by a true practitioner who has served fruitfully as a pastor, church planter, district and denominational leader, spiritual leader, and a dear friend. I have personally witnessed the principles of this book implemented. It works! *-Dr. Dan A. Berry, District Superintendent, author of "No More Cloudy Days".*

Dr. Dan Finch has succeeded in touching a throbbing nerve in the heart and life of most every pastor. Stories of many real-life situations in churches Finch himself has known carry the message of the struggles that a pastor, like Pastor Tom in the book, may experience. The whole purpose of this book is to give pastors a method of moving from "Dreams to Teams" in the church. The "Team-Up" challenge for moving people into the marketplace to win a lost world includes numerous outlines of sermons based on biblical people who changed their world. Easy to read, with a wealth of resources, pastors will grow with their church teams. -Wayne E. Caldwell, Th.D. Professor, Indiana Wesleyan University, 1972-2008 General Editor, *The Wesleyan Church*, 1984-1992

"Dan Finch's *Transfusion* is the distilled wisdom of a leader who's lived what he writes about...the joys, tears, mistakes, fears, and the eternal fruit that makes everything worth it. As I read Dan's book I found myself nodding often in understanding and agreement...so many of us have lived similar stories! You'll find *Transfusion* biblical, practical, inspirational, and especially adaptable and applicable. There's help and hope in this book. Let *Transfusion* infuse you with a fresh heart for your personal and ministry journey." -- Dr. Tim Roehl, Director of Training, One Mission Society Author, *TransforMisional Coaching* and *Game Plan*.

"Oh my friends, we are loaded down with countless church activities, while the real work of the church, that of evangelizing the world and winning the lost **is almost entirely neglected."** -Oswald J. Smith

SPECIAL THANKS TO

My dear wife, Carol Ann Finch, who has partnered with me in love and ministry from the time we launched the rebirth of the Sni Mills Community Holiness Church at Lone Jack, Missouri on June 23, 1957 until now.

Dr. John C. Maxwell, author, church growth leader, mentor, and friend who used Operation Outreach in his church and selected my church as a pilot church to launch the re-tooled G.R.A.D.E. Program.

Dr. Jerry Pence, former General Superintendent of the Wesleyan Church for encouraging me to write such a book to reintroduce G.R.A.D.E. as TEAM-UP EVANGELISM.

Dr. Kevin Myers, Senior Pastor at 12 Stone Church, whom I have had the awesome privilege and joy of working with and for over the past two decades.

Dr. Dan A. Berry, District Superintendent, who inspired the term Dream Summit and made Team-UP available to the churches on his district.

Kirk Kirlin for introducing me to the "Personal and Church Time-line" concepts

Stephen Bechdol for working with me to get the manuscript started.

Pat Edghill for a great job in formatting the Discipleship booklets for our classes to use.

And many others too numerous to mention.

To learn more about TEAM-*UP* Evangelism, visit
www.outskirtspress.com/transfusion
www.teamupevangelism.com

TABLE OF CONTENTS

CHAPTER ONE 1
PARKING LOT INTERCEPTION 1
GREEN TURNS TO GRAY... 2
THE GATHERING STORM... 5
SHATTERING NEWS... 7

CHAPTER TWO 11
FINAL GOODBYES.. 11
CHANGE OF DIRECTION 13
ENCOUNTER WITH GOD 15
SURRENDER 16
PEACE LIKE A RIVER 17

CHAPTER THREE 20
THE AWAKENING 20
LOW-GRADE SUSPICION 23
THE CONFERENCE THAT LEFT A BITTER TASTE27
LET THE MURMURING BEGIN 30
SOUL-WINNING FIASCO 32

CHAPTER FOUR..35
THE VISITOR... 35
THE TURNING POINT 40
SUMMER AT STARBUCKS 43
THE PASTOR GETS A NEW WIFE............................ 46

CHAPTER FIVE 48
CHURCH GROW EXPO EXPLOSION....................... 48
IN THE VALLEY OF THE SHADOW OF DIVISON. 52
INDECISION TIME... 53
HUMILITY TAKES CENTER STAGE 55

CHANGE POINT 58

CHAPTER SIX 60

PUTTING PRAYER FRONT AND CENTER 60

DISASTERS THAT KEEP ON HURTING 62

HEALING THE HEART OF THE CHURCH 65

THE BAPTISM 67

ONE LIFE-CHANGING STORY 68

CHAPTER SEVEN 73

WHAT A DIFFERENCE A YEAR MAKES 73

A NEW BEGINNING 75

A NEW STRATEGY TAKES SHAPE 76

THE SERMON SERIES THAT CHANGED EVERY-
THING 78

DREAMS TO TEAMS FAIR 78

BLAST-OFF 79

CHAPTER EIGHT 82

THE STORIES BEGIN 82

A PASTOR IN DISTRESS 84

WARNING SIGNS 84

THE FIERY FIVE 85

CHAPTER NINE 88

THE UNEXPECTED AND UNTHINKABLE
HAPPENS 88

AN UNLIKELY PLACE FOR A STAFF MEETING 89

LESSONS LEARNED FROM A HOSPITAL BED 89

THE SONG MUST GO ON 90

THE FIRST ORDER OF BUSINESS 91

CONCLUSION 95

DISCIPLESHIP BOOKLETS 95

FOREWORD

You have got to be kidding! Why release another book about evangelism on a market already flooded? Bookshelves are overflowing with plans, tools, and books designed to promote evangelism! But, why not? If people coming to faith in Christ is the heart of God, can there be too many books and articles about that? How important is spending all eternity with God when He "has planted eternity in the human heart....?" (Ecclesiastes 3:11 [NLT])

I wish the 80/20 principle applied to evangelism in the average church. If only 20% of the people were actively engaged in effective evangelism, the results would be huge! But the sad fact is that the percentage is so small in many places, it doesn't even exist. The great work of evangelism is often pushed aside in favor of scores of other well-intentioned projects and ministries.

How can a pastor help every believer in his church become involved in fulfilling the Great Commission? Or should he? Those are the piercing questions before us.

Recently I was reading from a book printed in 1922 only to discover that some of the pages had never been cut open since publication—when I did cut them open, I read these words: "The day I awoke from indifference and formality, the sounds of eternity came rushing like a cold, sharp east wind into my ears. I remember the day I woke; and the next day when I got the light....It is one thing to be awakened and another thing to get up." (Rev John McNeill)

On page 125 of the Cyclopedia of Twentieth Century Illustrations by Amos R. Wells Fleming, H. Revell Company, you will find these words. "Let churches learn a lesson. Hothouse Christianity tends to the elimination of seeds. There is constant danger that a church may become self-satisfied in its succulent prosperity, and lose its power of self-propagation. Let us get out from under glass, let us jump the fences, let us go forth into the high-ways, and make even the wilderness blossom as the rose!"

Carl F. H. Henry once wrote, "The prime need of the Church in these times is a new sense of its proper task."

As I have spent my life pastoring and also working with other pastors and churches, I have grown to understand more and more their struggles and dreams. I kept wondering how I could best serve the hundreds of churches and pastors across the land, who are frustrated when their dreams are unfulfilled. Then it hit me: Why not tell the story of one fictional pastor, and include many of the challenges I have seen pastors and churches face? Pastor Tom Bachman is that fictional pastor. St. Matthew's Church and Pleasant Valley, Iowa are that fictional church and place. The stories have been created, altered, adapted, and changed to fit the narrative. However, the Discipleship booklets and resource materials are real and have been used successfully in hundreds of churches.

All across the country there are many pastors and churches who need a "TRANSFUSION" of hope, vision, and spiritual energy. Journey with Pastor Tom Bachman and St. Matthew's Church as they search for a new spiritual "transfusion" to be on map and on mission to build the Kingdom of Christ.

It is my humble prayer that this little book will be used by God to awaken His church to the great opportunity of reaching as many people as possible for Christ and His Kingdom.

CHAPTER ONE

PARKING LOT INTERCEPTION

It was the last thing he wanted on his first day off in two weeks! Pastor Tom Bachman was headed out for a long-overdue day at the golf course. But dark anger clutched around his neck as he turned onto the parking lot of St. Matthew's Church to drop off his sermon outline for next Sunday's bulletin. There was no mistake about who was behind the wheel of the approaching shiny black sedan. This soft-spoken but extremely irritating man was always trying to snag Pastor Tom about some prayer retreat or spiritual life conference. An encounter with Steve Crenshaw would dismally invade the rest of his day like a severe case of poison ivy, oozing and irritating. Pastor Tom frantically thought about possible escape routes to avoid another one of Steve's nagging "spiritual consultations." He could do a 180-degree turn, leaving Steve in total bewilderment as to what emergency he was suddenly called away to. Or he could pretend he didn't see Steve at all and make a mad dash into the church.

"It's no use," he mumbled. "I might as well park and at least act like a pastor. Even though sometimes I don't feel like one, especially today," he muttered under his breath.

It was at times like this that an ugly darkness rose up in his soul, demanding a reason as to why he was even in the ministry in the first place. And, as before, there was no time to respond. He simply got out of his car and strode briskly toward the office door.

"Hey, Pastor, I am so glad to catch up with you today," came that irritating voice, cutting like a sharp knife through the peace of an otherwise beautiful spring morning as Steve sprinted to reach Pastor Tom.

"Well," Pastor Tom curtly replied, "I'm really in a hurry. Maybe we can talk some other time. I was just stopping by the office for a brief moment to drop something off. I am already late for a very important engagement." (*Yes, golf is important*, he mused to himself).

"Don't worry; this will take only a minute." There was that unwelcome, irritating voice again. As Steve briskly approached, Pastor Tom winced at the sight of the colorful brochure in his already outstretched hand.

GREEN TURNS TO GRAY

As Pastor Tom drove through the rolling countryside on Highway 23, he realized he hadn't played golf since before the holidays. Winter had held an ugly grip on the weather around Pleasant Valley for far too long. In fact, he mused, there had been little time for anything except the stress and strain of church, ministry, and family.

The last five months had been extremely difficult. Back in October he had been called upon to mediate a dispute between his brother and wife as their marriage unraveled. Tom had always been envious of his brother. Seeing his brother's pain awakened conflicting emotions in him, including guilt over his lifelong jealousy of his brother's achievements.

Then on Christmas Eve, his mother had died unexpectedly. This renewed again the sense of loss and emptiness he had experienced when his father had died in a plane crash some twenty-five years earlier. His eyes began to water unexpectedly as he thought about the last time he had seen his mother's sweet smile. Through good times and bad, she was always his greatest cheerleader. He had called and visited her as often as possible. Now it was hard to believe that she was gone. He missed her more than words could say.

And now there was Larry. Years ago and a thousand miles away in Weatherford, Pastor Tom and Larry had been high school buddies. They had played on the high school golf team and chased girls together. They had been roommates in college before Pastor Tom went on to seminary. Over the years, hundreds of miles separated them and they eventually lost touch.

It had been a pleasant surprise three years ago when Pastor Tom and his family moved to Pleasant Valley, only to discover that Larry and Joan were living there! He had been transferred by his job ten years previously, and had established himself in the community. It didn't take long for Tom and Larry to return to their golf partnership on the greens.

Soon after Tom became pastor at St. Matthew's, Larry's wife Joan began attending the church, but Larry always had an excuse for not coming with her. Once or twice he had shown up for Christmas and Easter services, but he was vocally adamant that religion in any form was not for him. Tom had many things in common with Larry—football, hunting, and fast cars; however, God, faith, and religion were always avoided in the conversations.

Normally Larry would have been with Tom on this trip

to the Bedford Greens Golf Course, but not today. Larry was in the hospital. It had been just two weeks since Larry's day was suddenly interrupted with a heart attack in the middle of the executive meeting of the Green Valley Tool and Die Company. When Pastor Tom met Joan at the hospital, she told him of Larry's recurring heart problem. It had led to borderline diabetes and was complicated by lung cancer. Much of this was related to Larry's heavy smoking habit ever since high school.

Pastor Tom's hospital visit had been brief. With some of his parishioners, he would have ended with a short prayer of hope and blessing, but this was Larry. Tom felt awkward to venture beyond the invisible boundaries that excluded faith and God, which Larry had set throughout the years of their friendship. He felt he must respect Larry's feelings too much to offend his old golfing buddy. So he had left with only a wave of the hand and a "see you later."

As Tom drove on toward the golf course, he reminisced about his last visit with Larry at New Haven Regional Medical Center, just three days before. Larry was propped up in bed, his face almost as pale as the pillows.

"How is it going today?" Pastor Tom asked with a forced smile.

"I'd rather be golfing," Larry responded, barely opening his eyes.

The two began to exchange pleasantries and soon turned to their favorite round of humor and oft-told sports jokes. Again he left without saying a prayer, or any talk about God.

On his way home that day, Tom remembered he had stopped by the New Line Electronics store on Jenkins Highway. He loved gadgets—old and new—and he needed something to get his mind off Larry's condition. The more he thought about Larry, the more concerned he became. What if Larry didn't pull through this illness? How would Joan and the kids cope? How would *he* cope with losing his friend?

Leaving the TV section, Tom was walking through the middle of the bass-thumping stereos when he felt the vibration of his cell phone. The message was urgent. Larry had gone into cardiac arrest. So Tom had rushed back to the hospital, spending the night with the distraught family. But Larry had pulled through the immediate crisis. The doctor reported that the odds were in Larry's favor, but it would take time, patience, and plenty of prayer for a full recovery. Dr. Stockton was known in the area as the doctor who wasn't afraid to talk about God or even pray with his patients before surgery.

For a moment Tom wondered about his own hesitancy to talk about God with people who had no faith. What did the doctor have that he didn't?

"Why don't I have that kind of courage?" he mused to himself. "Is it because my own faith falters under pressure, or because I don't know what to say?"

Driving on toward the Bedford Greens Golf Course, Tom pondered his own faith journey, feeling ashamed and convicted. But he was going to golf, and that was that.

THE GATHERING STORM

Near the end of the 45-minute drive north, the skies began to open up to a warm fragrance-filled spring day. Pastor Tom had longed for this opportunity to get away from everything—his personal grief over the loss of his mother, those annoying parishioners, the hospital visits, the rowdy children, the long hours of study and church administration. For Pastor Tom, golf had always been his way to escape both the monotony and stress of everyday life. It had helped him work out multiple frustrations. Golf was his "spiritual therapy."

"I need golf; I deserve golf," he sighed to himself. "After all I have gone through this winter, I have earned a full, uninterrupted day of nothing but golf and pure relaxation!"

As Tom turned off the main road and began to wind up the road to the Bedford Greens Clubhouse, he still felt irritated about the last appointment of the previous day with Carmen Broyles. It was beginning to appear that Carmen, Steve, and a small group of other "super saints" in the church had joined forces to point out all his spiritual shortcomings. He wondered why people who claimed to be so spiritual sometimes appeared to be so cruel. Didn't they have anything better to do than to attack pastors? He was always coming up short in their eyes in one way or another. And his only response was a defensive attitude.

When the appointment had ended, Pastor Tom felt like he had been shot full of holes. He had hurried home--late for supper, as usual. His children had already finished eating and were busy with their homework. Again, his problems at the church had overshadowed his responsibilities at home. He always seemed to be busy with church stuff when his children needed him most. His perceived failure as a father wildly overwhelmed him. Darkness clutched relentlessly at his soul!

With great effort Tom pushed all those thoughts out of his mind and began to golf.

SHATTERING NEWS

When Pastor Tom got to the first hole, he started swinging with new resolve. Birdie—*Not bad*, he thought. *I haven't played in so long, but I still have the touch.* As he continued through the subsequent sand traps and ball-hunting expeditions, he began to relax and breathe deeply the warm fragrant spring air under the deep brilliant blue sky. Steve, Carmen, and Larry were all hidden under the blanket of a distant memory. Yes, Tom was feeling better.

As Tom approached the 5th hole, the afternoon's peace and quiet was shattered by the nerve-racking ring of his cell phone. "Why didn't I turn that thing off before I came out here?" he grumbled to himself. Ignoring the ring, Tom clenched his teeth in a momentary burst of anger and took a solid swing at the golf ball. As his eyes followed its long arc against the blue sky, he realized it had gone far off course to the right.

"Great! Wish I had a caddy...." he mused as he looked down to see who his unwelcome caller was. Under his breath, he couldn't help but mutter a few choice words of frustration about his inept staff for their inconsiderate interruption. They had been instructed not to call him.

Tom finished all nine holes and went to the clubhouse to drink a soda before checking his voicemail. Sue, his administrative assistant, had received a call from Joan Duncan. She had asked if Pastor Tom could stop by the hospital to pay a visit to her husband, Larry. Larry was not doing well and the family thought a visit from his old high school buddy and current golfing partner would cheer him up.

Pastor Tom resented this interruption on his day off, even

though it was a call to visit his old friend. He wondered what was so important now that it couldn't wait until tomorrow. He wondered why Larry's family was leaning on him so hard to do what for him was becoming increasingly difficult to do.

Begrudgingly, Pastor Tom started the drive south toward the hospital. As he traveled, he couldn't help but notice the dark clouds beginning to form low on the western horizon. They were beginning to remind him too much of his own life. Gradually a haunting agony deep within was making his life unbearable. He was bored and unfulfilled with his ministry. Wasn't there something more than the endless monotony of meetings, counseling, and sermons? Suddenly he realized that the excitement of ministry was fading away, if he had ever really had it. He had no joy, no surging energy to continue. For a moment the thought whisked through his mind of doing something else with his life. *Maybe, just maybe I could….*and his thoughts trailed off into oblivion. His mind went numb the next few minutes.

As Pastor Tom approached Grand Haven Regional Hospital, once again his thoughts wandered back to the recent Easter service. Everything had come together without a hitch. Several dozen visitors, more than usual, had shown up at St. Matthew's. Everyone was in their best attire, the choir had sounded great, and Tom was quite proud of his Easter sermon. From a pastor's perspective, the service couldn't have been better.

Even Larry had come, and commented upon leaving that he had enjoyed the service. Now, as he approached the hospital, Pastor Tom wondered why something about that service kept gnawing at his spirit. It had seemed so successful… but something was wrong? Something was missing! What was it? That question was beginning to haunt him more and more.

As Pastor Tom turned to walk down the hall on the 3rd floor where Larry was in ICU, his heart seemed to skip a beat and his hands became clammy. Up ahead he saw Larry's family gathered in a huddle outside the door. Faces were drawn and somber. The doctor was standing there motionless. Joan's face was buried in her father's chest. He could hear the unmistakable sound of sobbing. Something was terribly wrong.

He whispered a brief prayer and quickened his pace. As much as he had tried to prepare himself for the worst scenario, he couldn't have prepared himself for what he was about to hear. Joan looked up and gasped, "Larry's gone." Time stood still.

QUESTIONS FOR REFLECTION

TRANSFUSION: The Nagging of a Faithful Conscience Begins to Awaken the Heart of a Slumbering Pastor.

1. What do you think Pastor Tom was trying to avoid in his life and ministry?
2. What are some ways God awakens people spiritually?
3. In what ways do misplaced priorities keep us from doing God's will?
4. What causes us to be blind to spiritual realities?

CHAPTER TWO

FINAL GOODBYES

A wave of guilt flooded over Pastor Tom as he drove on home from the hospital. His friend had lain dying, a family needed him, yet he had been so consumed with his own self-centered pursuits that he wouldn't even stop his golf game long enough to answer his phone, let alone rush to help. Could he have made it to the hospital in time? He struggled with the aching loss of his longtime friend and school chum. The darkness within deepened.

Between guilt and loss, Tom felt like he was sleepwalking the next few days. He spent time with the family, worked on a eulogy, did routine tasks, but nothing seemed real. He went through the motions of what was expected of him as a pastor, but he felt like a bystander to the action. He spent time with the grieving family, but could do little for them because of his own guilt and devastation. He came up woefully short when trying to answer questions about the afterlife. Guilt swept over his soul like a frigid north wind.

Even though everyone spoke of Larry being in a better place, there was that dark cloud hanging low, robbing Tom of that assurance. Larry had never made it a secret that he did not believe in God the way Christians said they believed. But Larry seemed to have it together, despite God not being in his life. What could Tom say in the eulogy? How could he offer hope and ease the pain of loss to the family—especially Joan—when his own soul was wrenched by the agony of the unspoken?

During the visitation the night before the funeral service, Pastor Tom looked down at Larry's face in the casket. Extreme and unsettling questions, along with nagging doubts, began to flood his mind. He had known Larry for years, but they had never discussed how to get ready for heaven. He had been such a coward, and so afraid of offending Larry. He was afraid that conversations about spiritual things would dampen or damage their relationship. He was just afraid. And now he knew that kind of behavior toward a friend was totally unacceptable. As he leaned in closer by the casket, he pondered Larry's destiny.

Larry had been in church for the Easter service just a few weeks earlier. What a missed opportunity! Tom recalled how he had generalized the Resurrection story but said little of a personal faith in Christ. But how could he? Graduating from Parkwood Seminary with its liberal professors, he had tried hard to avoid identification with evangelical Christianity. His theology was based on a positive mental attitude that embraced all people as God's children and said little if anything about Christ dying on the cross. If people believed in God and tried to be as good as they could, then somehow they would all get to heaven in the end.

But staring death in the face caused Tom to question the validity of all he had tried weakly to believe about Christ and Christianity. There was no mistake about it; Larry was dead, and Tom was faced with the consequences of his own failure as a spiritual guide.

The funeral of his friend Larry Duncan was one of the worst experiences of Pastor Tom's life so far. The church was packed. Larry was well-liked by many both in his company and the community. They all came to pay their final respects. Pastor Tom stumbled through the service with vague references to God and heaven. He felt responsible to say more—to do more, but he was trapped by his own guilt and fear.

But it wasn't until the last few moments of standing around the casket that the full truth of his empty theology hit him hard in the face. As he saw Joan and the Duncan children lean over the casket weeping their final goodbyes— he knew it really was the final goodbye! They had no hope of seeing him again! Larry died without knowing how to go to heaven, and Tom was stricken by an overwhelming sense of guilt and shame. Deep within, Tom thought he had known the answer all along, but only now admitted his personal spiritual failure. As he walked before the casket out of the church, he sensed his own life was about to take an abrupt turn.

CHANGE OF DIRECTION

How he ever managed to get home after the funeral and the graveside committal Tom would never know. But there he was sitting at his own kitchen table. His shoulders slumped and his countenance was dark. His sad eyes looked far away without seeing anything.

Sandra appeared in the doorway and said, "Hi, Tom— how did the funeral go? Do you want me to pour you a cup of coffee?" He did not reply. He was unable to speak because he was thinking thoughts too dark to repeat. At that moment, he was considering his options. He had just let a wonderful human being slip through his fingers into an eternal night without God! He was ready to abandon the ministry and run away as fast and hard as he could. A thick fog penetrated his spirit, disabling any sense of direction or reason. He could not continue. Something had to give.

But what? What was wrong? He had attended the recommended seminary of his denomination. Although not the most brilliant in his class, he had graduated with honors. He had followed the prescribed church system and paid his ministerial dues. Until recently, he thought he somewhat enjoyed his job. He loved the strokes of being needed and depended-on by people in his congregations and communities. Yet something had always been gnawing away at his soul like a beaver bringing down a tree. The loss of his friend, Larry, was the straw that broke the camel's back. Something had to be done, but what?

"Day after tomorrow is Sunday," Pastor Tom moaned, realizing with a start that it would be up to him to say something spiritually profound to the congregation. For the past three years he had served the St. Matthew's parish. Through the week he had offered hope to the hurting and on Sunday he had delivered a well-crafted twenty-minute sermon…or was it a talk? He had avoided controversial issues. People had often congratulated him because they said his sermons made them feel good.

But St. Matthew's was his third pastorate and he was beginning to feel bored, wondering if he was ready for a change. He had always thought of St. Matthew's as a stepping stone to a bigger, well-known large city church where his legacy would be written. As a matter of fact, he was beginning to resent St. Matthew's because it was so small and located in rural, sleepy Pleasant Valley.

"Honey," Tom said as he broke the long silence, "remember that cabin on Blue Lake that Joe and Sally own? I'm going to call and see if I can go down there for a few days after Sunday services. I need some time alone. There are some things I need to sort out."

ENCOUNTER WITH GOD

Dashing home after an exhausting Sunday morning, it didn't take Tom long to throw some clothes in his travel bag, kiss Sandra goodbye, and hit the road. As he drove he mused, "How do you begin an encounter with God? How do you hear God's voice? Will He really speak to me?" He had brought his Bible, along with two other books he had been trying to find time to read. "Would reading these books be the place to begin?"

When Pastor Tom reached the cabin, he threw his things inside, found a sturdy walking stick, and set out to hike around the lake, eventually moving into the woods beyond. With every step, his anguish of spirit washed over him with unrelenting intensity. How could he forgive himself for failing his friend Larry? How could God ever forgive him for such gross negligence, letting a man die without knowing the power of God's forgiveness? What was the crooked trail he had followed so blindly that had brought him to such irresponsibility?

Tom found a large rock on a cliff and dropped down to rest. He pulled a small Bible from his pocket and began to read. As he read, he began to re-evaluate his life and ministry in the light of scripture. It was as if God were holding a 10,000-watt light, exposing his soul. The more he read, the more he realized his emptiness and hopelessness. He fell on his knees and cried out in great distress.

SURRENDER

Two hours later when Tom returned to the cabin, he decided to sit on the front porch swing and read one of the books that he had brought with him. It was a paperback edition of the *Life of John Wesley* by Basil Miller, given to him by a member in his very first church. He had always admired Wesley, and as he read he began to identify with him. For years, Wesley had preached out of a sense of duty, but without the assurance of salvation. He had traveled to America to preach to the Native Americans, but was woefully unsuccessful. Story after story about Wesley's life and ministry reached out to Tom. On page 61, he read the account of Mr. Wesley's Aldersgate experience--where his "heart was strangely warmed"--Tom could stand it no longer. What Larry had died without knowing, and what he was missing, was exactly what John Wesley had. Wesley talked about how he knew he had a personal relationship with Jesus. Tom thought, *That's the very thing I need to know.*

There on the porch that afternoon, Tom fell to his knees and buried his head. He could not go on without knowing he was forgiven and had the assurance of eternal salvation.

He cried out, "Larry, I am so sorry. God, please forgive me. I need to be changed!"

For several minutes, Pastor Tom confessed his sins to

God. He felt a wave of sorrow washing over his soul like a creek in flood stage as he thought of his spiritual failures. He asked God to forgive him for being a ho-hum Christian in name only. A Bible verse he had memorized as a child came racing out of the past. Out loud Pastor Tom quoted the words, which now burst alive with new meaning.

Matthew 11:28-30: "Come unto Me, all ye that labor and are heavy laden, and I will give you rest. Take My yoke upon you, and learn of Me; for I am meek and lowly in heart; and ye shall find rest unto your souls. For My yoke is easy, and My burden is light."

Tom was coming to Christ on bended knee, seeking forgiveness.

PEACE LIKE A RIVER

What happened next was the watershed moment that would forever change his life. As he cried out, "Lord, I believe, come live within me, I make you my Lord and Savior," he was so strongly filled with wonder and awe that it nearly overwhelmed him. In the church where he grew up he remembered singing out of the "Waves of Glory" No. 2 hymnal. The words of one song suddenly came back to him,

"Peace, Peace, Wonderful Peace" he began to sing,
"Coming down from the Father above!
Sweep over my spirit forever, I pray,
In fathomless billows of love."

Suddenly he remembered a verse so long forgotten. He

sang lustily,

> "Far away in the depths of my spirit tonight
> Rolls a melody sweeter than psalm.
> In celestial like strains, it unceasingly falls,
> O'er my spirit like an infinite calm."

Then it seemed the song came gushing out. The presence of the Lord seemed to totally envelop him. He felt cleansed and healed within. He knew beyond a shadow of doubt that he was really forgiven. He nearly shouted another verse,

> "What a treasure I have in this wonderful peace,
> Buried deep in the heart of my soul,
> So secure that no power can mine it away,
> While the years of eternity roll!"

Suddenly for the first time in all his forty-five years, Tom knew what the peace of God was really like. He absolutely knew that he, Tom Bachman was newly alive in Christ. He understood now what so many others had already experienced and testified to in their lives. For the first time, he was filled with a new *"transfusion"* of joy and assurance of salvation and an overwhelming sense of God's unconditional love. For the first time in a long time, Pastor Tom was glad to be alive. Tom Bachman would never be the same again!

QUESTIONS FOR REFLECTION

TRANSFUSION: Many Different Circumstances Combine Together to Bring About a Much-Needed Heart Change in the Pastor

1. What would have happened if Pastor Tom had buried his feelings of guilt rather than facing them?
2. How did the events of death and loss speak to Pastor Tom?
3. How does God convict us of sin and disobedience?
4. What is your definition of conversion?

CHAPTER THREE

THE AWAKENING

What an incredible week! In the solitude of the cabin by the lake and the woods, Pastor Tom had spent the entire time in the boxing ring with God and was soundly knocked out in the final round. God had won! Tom's ministerial arrogance was fading away like the morning mist under the encroaching rays of the rising sun, and he knew how Moses must have felt standing before God on holy ground at the burning bush. As Pastor Tom saw himself in the light of God's absolute holiness and goodness, he had to face the fact that he was a living example of religious hypocrisy. He thought he knew all the right phrases, the right theology, but somehow he had missed out on knowing about a right relationship with God. He had known about God, but he did not know God!

Symbolically, he took off his shoes and fell prostrate as he continued to think and pray about his life and ministry. Tomorrow would be his final day at the cabin. He knew he wasn't yet ready to leave. He still had some more unfinished business with God.

On Friday morning, Pastor Tom awoke early and walked briskly to the lake. Hiking alone along the shoreline in the early light of the sunrise, he was reminded of the scene when Peter and John met Jesus on the shore of Lake Galilee. In his mind's eye he could almost see Peter and John mending their nets in sorrow because they thought Jesus was dead. Suddenly it was as if he could also see Jesus unexpectedly appearing in person, standing on the shore not far from a charcoal fire.

Gripped by the scene in his mind, it was as if *he* were identifying with Peter as Peter heard the question of Christ.

"Peter, do you love Me?"

Boastfully, Peter leaned over to Christ to confirm his unfailing devotion for the Lord, "O, yes, Lord, I love you most of all."

"Do you really, truly love Me, Peter?" Christ asked again.

Peter was surprised at the repeated question.

"Of course I love You. And Jesus, I am so glad You are with us again. I was scared You were gone forever."

"Then, take care of my sheep!" Jesus spoke with a faraway sadness that seemed to dampen the morning calm. Without relenting and for the third time Jesus asked the same question He had asked before.

"Peter, do you love Me?"

By now, Peter was offended. How could Jesus doubt his undying devotion?

Pastor Tom didn't hear Peter's final response because Christ's questions were driven like an arrow deeply into his now troubled, but awakened spirit. He was beginning to see how he was only marking time in ministry. What he had counted as success—increased attendance, increased budgets—was only an effort to feed his ego and receive kudos from his denomination. But tragically, he had missed the mark of leading his churches to be lighthouses of hope and faith to their respective communities. In fact, he had not personally guided anyone to receive Christ and be baptized since he had been at St. Matthew's.

Tears began to flow unbidden as Pastor Tom fell to his knees in deep spiritual remorse. He saw that he, like Peter, had boasted superficial devotion to Christ, only to deny Him when it mattered most. He had denied Christ by giving only lip service to loving and serving Him. He, Tom Bachman, had denied Christ every time he visited Larry and others by not showing them how they could come to faith in Christ. He had denied Jesus every time he had preached a sermon without mentioning the cross, the need for repentance, or forgiveness. He had denied Christ over and over again with empty words and actions. He had been robbing people of their right to know God personally.

The longer he prayed, the more he realized that he had miserably missed the whole point of ministry. Not only had he been a casual Christian drifting along as a minister, but he had been dishing out lame recipes of self-help in the place of eternal realities. He had not helped hurting and hungry people discover new hope and life in Jesus Christ.

Weeping softly, he grasped the impossibility of bringing Larry back from the grave. There would be no second chance for his best friend. He understood how fatally he had blown it with Larry, and that he would never see him again. He also knew that he was now forgiven of his lifelong gross negligence. All those failures were in the past. He knew he needed to press forward with a new spiritual vigor. From now on he would do his best to reach as many people as possible with the wonderful news that Jesus could change their life. There would be other Larrys, and that ignited a new resolution.

"I promise you, Larry, I will never let anyone else die in

my world without doing my best to point them to Christ."

Pastor Tom's voice was certain--and his heart was so light, and finally right. It had been a long week: a week of battles, discoveries, and victories. Tom jogged quickly back to the cabin, consumed with a new passion. He had a love for Christ that he had never known before. He had transitioned from being a Martha "busy here and there" to a Mary "sitting in rapture at the feet of Jesus." He had become a student of the Master and was he ever learning. He knew his mission. From now on he would be telling people about Jesus and what He had to offer.

It was time to head back to his family and St. Matthew's.

LOW-GRADE SUSPICION

Pastor Tom couldn't wait to get home and share with Sandra everything that had happened. All during the week of his extreme encounter with God, he had kept wondering how Sandra would react to his story. She had grown up in a non-Christian home and was never very religious. They had met during their college years and she had expressed her reluctance for him to go on to seminary and pursue a career with the church. However, Sandra was everything anybody would expect to be as a model preacher's wife—loving, good, and compassionate.

Tom couldn't wait to rehearse for Sandra his week, recounting every moment of his incredible spiritual adventure. He knew he would never forget the experience of meeting God at that lakeside cabin. All Friday evening and again on Saturday morning, they talked. She was curious and distant, but not overly excited. The difference in Tom could not be denied, yet it was still something she could not understand. Something had happened to her husband and she knew he was forever changed. She secretly began to wonder about her own need for spiritual change.

When Saturday afternoon came, Pastor Tom knew it was time to head to St. Matthew's to plan how he would address his congregation the next morning. How do you tell people you have had a "burning bush" encounter? How do you describe the awesomeness of God's Presence? How do you tell your congregation the truth about your failure to be their spiritual guide? How do you ask forgiveness of the people who call you their pastor and shepherd?

The more he mused about the right approach to take, the more he realized that his description of his life-changing week would be difficult for some people to understand. It might even make some people uncomfortable. In fact, the very thought of what he ought to say and had to say made Tom uncomfortable as well. In the past, Pastor Tom would have acknowledged his thoughts and feelings—maybe—but his pride would have caused him to be defensive. He would have tried to explain away the supernatural with the natural. Now in his new state of humility, he was willing to bare his heart in honest confession. He wanted to put himself aside and exalt Jesus Christ.

"Perhaps," he mused, "that was what John the Baptist meant when he said, 'Christ must increase and I must decrease.'"

Before returning home on Saturday evening, Pastor Tom went into the old but well- maintained stately sanctuary of St. Matthew's and knelt down at the communion rail. Looking up at the giant wooden cross above the choir seats, he realized that he was actually excited about preaching in the morning. It shocked him, because he had never anticipated Sunday with such expectancy. Throughout his ministry, Sunday had been a day like all the other work days in his clergy job; but tonight he was expecting the movement of God in this very place tomorrow!

As the service progressed the next morning, Pastor Tom could hardly contain himself. He worshipped like he had never worshipped before. He lost himself in the music. He was drawn into the Presence of God in fresh and unexpected ways. The songs were all the old-time church favorites, but singing them today brought new meaning for him.

When the time came for Pastor Tom to speak, he moved away from the pulpit and with Bible in hand came down in front of the congregation. He was overwhelmed with a deep love and compassion that made him want to get as close to the people as possible. For the first time he saw the congregation of St. Matthew's like Jesus had been seeing it all along. Until today they had been sheep without a shepherd. But that was about to change.

For the next twenty minutes, Pastor Tom poured out his story about the events of the week at the cabin. He told about reading the story of John Wesley's conversion and his own newfound relationship with God. He recounted how he had fallen to his knees on the front porch of the cabin and experienced a forgiveness and peace like he had never known before. He told how he wrestled with God like Jacob in the Bible all week long, yielding his life to God in new and fresh ways. As he walked back and forth across the front of the sanctuary, his words were unscripted, but filled with passion and sincerity. As he described his "cabin by the lake" experience, some responded by weeping silently;

others looked puzzled. He confessed his shortcomings and rejoiced in his newly discovered joy, love, and hope in the Lord. Along with his confessions and vivid testimony came Pastor Tom's pledge that since the church now had a renewed pastor, he felt God was asking him to lead them in a new direction. With firm confidence, Pastor Tom declared that St. Matthew's should be a loving church—a church that reached spiritually unresolved people for Christ.

When the people were leaving after the service, Pastor Tom heard some voice their appreciation for his authenticity and honesty. They seemed to approve of his newfound commitment for God and St. Matthew's. But Pastor Tom could also sense that others didn't know quite what to make of their pastor's change of direction and behavior. Others were distant and outright skeptical.

By Monday morning, the phone lines were hot with discussions and suspicions about the pastor's new emotionalism. What was this "Moses experience" all about? Theories spread about what had happened to Pastor Tom. Had he been entranced by a false and unwise religious group? Had he finally wilted under the pressures of life and had an emotional breakdown? But there were a few who secretly knew what had truly happened to Pastor Tom and they were filled with joy and gratitude to God for answered prayer.

Along with all the theories that circulated through the community, the common consent of some was that "we liked the old Pastor Tom much better." "The old Pastor Tom never made us uncomfortable; he preached only feel-good messages." They felt that anybody could depend on him to be the rock in the midst of crises and turmoil. He had been emotionally stable and very likeable. But this new Pastor

Tom appeared to be just the opposite. The consensus was that this change was suspicious. Maybe something should be done. But what?

THE CONFERENCE THAT LEFT A BITTER TASTE

Early Monday morning, Pastor Tom went to his office with more excitement than he could ever remember. In the past, Monday had been just another work day. Yet on this day, it was different. Tom was full of ideas. Today, he had an unbridled enthusiasm for what was about to happen. He had a passion for God that he had never known before.

His morning started off better than he had ever remembered. For the first time in a long time, he had read the Scriptures and prayed to God not out of duty, but out of a new spiritual hunger and desire. He actually *wanted* to read the Bible! He *wanted* to talk to God! He was more in love with God now than he had ever been in love with anybody. His greatest passion was to serve the Lord well.

As Pastor Tom eased down in the big black chair behind his antique maple desk, he glanced out the second-story window of his office. Looking down through the leaves of a giant white oak tree at the freshly mowed lawn, he remembered his first days at St. Matthew's. He had fallen in love with that view from the beginning. He remembered thinking, *What a perfect place to work and study.*

For a few minutes, as he sat there dreaming about the future of St. Matthew's, he noticed how the hedge of flaming red azalea bushes bordering the sidewalk had just come into full bloom. Pondering the oak tree and the bushes, he thought about the hundreds of people he had watched walk that sidewalk in rain and shine during his years as pastor. It occurred to him that he had missed so many opportunities to reach out to them.

"Where do I begin to bring about change in this church?" he wondered to himself.

"Sue," Pastor Tom called his administrative assistant on the phone intercom. "Could you get me the information on the Symposium on Evangelism out of the last issue of *Preacher's Weekly*?"

After reading the description of the conference, it didn't take Pastor Tom long to sign up online. Thinking back about the churches he had attended as a child, he realized they were far too busy keeping all their programs going for their own members to have time to worry about people *outside* the church. And the people in the churches he had served were far more concerned with their social calendars than the eternal destinies of their friends. Pastor Tom realized he knew very little about evangelism. He would change that! He was determined St. Matthew's would soon blaze a new trail to reach the unreached.

The very next week, it was time to make the trip to Chicago for the symposium. Except for the brief description in the magazine, Pastor Tom really didn't know what to expect. He had heard about McCormick's Place, the symposium's venue, but knew little about the organization putting on the event.

When he arrived, he was overwhelmed by the mere size of the crowds. He didn't know where to start because there were so many different exhibitions from different companies and organizations. After wandering around the concourse for an hour, filling his bag with promo materials,

Pastor Tom went into the auditorium and settled into his seat.

For two and a half days, he listened to lectures and stories, and learned about various methods of evangelism in the local church. Most of the talks were focused on different strategies to carry out evangelism. But the question that kept haunting him went unanswered—"How do you prepare a church to do evangelism?"

He came away from the symposium with the conclusion that real Christians would be thrilled at the opportunity to learn how to share their faith with those who don't know Christ. After all, he knew how he personally felt now about sharing his faith with non-believers. All he needed were the tools to get the job done.

The next Sunday, Pastor Tom boldly announced that he felt God was calling on St. Matthew's to go in a new direction—St. Matthew's should be a church that would focus on reaching the unchurched. Even then he should have noticed that the "amens" were few and far between.

"May 16th will mark the beginning of a new era at St. Matthew's—a season of winning the community for Christ." Acting on what he had heard some churches do, he declared, "Every Tuesday night will be designated as Evangelism Night.

"Be here promptly at 7:00," he continued. "I will begin by giving about fifteen minutes of training and then we will spread out and begin our work. We will visit homes and present the Plan of Salvation. Please rearrange your schedules and free up your Tuesday nights so you can be a part of reaching our community. I expect everyone to be here—no exceptions."

Throughout his message, Pastor Tom excitedly shared

many of the ideas presented at the symposium. The speakers had made it sound so simple. He just knew they could not fail.

"I challenge everyone here to become active in evangelism," Pastor Tom exhorted as he concluded his message. "God expects you and me to win our family, friends, and neighbors to Christ. Starting a week from Tuesday, you will have the perfect opportunity to fulfill the Great Commission, so come on out and become a witness for Christ."

LET THE MURMURING BEGIN

Pastor Tom thought he had done a good job of presenting his idea of how the church could do evangelism effectively, but it wasn't long before he heard people mumbling under their breath.

"Tuesday is my bowling night."

"Who is going to babysit the kids?"

"I am too tired after work to come to church on Tuesday."

"What about the Ladies' Missionary Auxiliary?"

Ah, yes…and the Ladies' Auxiliary. Pastor Tom had been a lukewarm supporter of this social event each week. He had never quite understood the purpose of several older ladies getting together to sing, talk, play games, and sew. To him, the way it was conducted was a waste of time.

It didn't take long, however, for Pastor Tom to be reminded that the auxiliary had gathered for years on Tuesdays. It was made up of some of the most influential ladies in the church, and they would not give up their night easily.

Monday morning, Pastor Tom met with the president of the auxiliary, Margaret Stenson. He was firm as he told her that the auxiliary would simply have to move to another time in the week or risk being dissolved so full participation could be gained in the new evangelism program. Margaret was indignant.

"Pastor Tom, the Ladies' Missionary Auxiliary has met for over twenty-four years on Tuesday night. Do you think you can whisk in here and expect us to simply give up our night so you can carry on some new-fangled idea that we really don't need here? Well, I tell you this, if you expect us to give up without a fight, you don't know what you are in for!"

With that, she slammed the door behind her. The battle lines had been drawn.

Only a few hours later, Pastor Tom received a call from Clyde Barnes, Chairman of the Board of Elders.

"I just got off the phone with Margaret," Clyde informed Pastor Tom with obvious irritation in his voice. "What do you think you are doing, telling her you are considering disbanding the Ladies' Missionary Auxiliary if they don't move the night of their meeting? Do you realize this group has been the backbone of St. Matthew's for years, besides being the only social event for most of those ladies? What will they do if they don't have the auxiliary?"

The phone call went on for a few minutes, but Pastor Tom firmly held his ground. His decision had been made. "They can find another time, or we will have to discontinue the organization."

SOUL-WINNING FIASCO

The week continued with countless threatening phone calls and even a signed petition. Despite everything, Pastor Tom pressed forward. When Sunday came, he reaffirmed Tuesday evening to be the "Outreach Night for Soul Winning." Pastor Tom reinforced what he said by pointing to the announcement in the bulletin.

"Meet me in the fellowship hall promptly at 7:00 p.m. We will begin with fifteen minutes of training. After a brief prayer, assignments will be given to each one and we will go up and down the streets of Pleasant Valley to share Christ. Everyone is expected to come—no exceptions."

As Tuesday night arrived, Pastor Tom went to church brimming over with excitement. He expected at least fifty people to be present, but no one came. He waited and waited. 7:15 came, then 7:30…nobody. Pastor Tom couldn't believe it. Not a living soul showed up! Boiling over with betrayal and anger, he turned out the lights just before 8:00 p.m. and went home.

"People can find time to go to the mall or the ball game, but they can't spend even one night walking up and down the street for God," Pastor Tom fumed to his wife Sandra, later that evening.

"What is wrong with these people?" For the rest of the week, Pastor Tom thought and planned what he would say to the congregation on Sunday morning.

Next Sunday wasn't pretty. Pastor Tom's anger charged the atmosphere with a new tension, unknown before. He lashed out at the congregation for their obvious cold-hearted apathy and lack of commitment. His words were caustic and biting. The peace that used to pervade the services at

St. Matthew's was gone. They cringed under Pastor Tom's scathing remarks.

Pastor Tom's Sunday-morning rebuke was met with open resistance. The few that supported Pastor Tom collided headlong with the majority who stood their ground against him with strong antagonism. This controversy caused great unrest throughout the congregation. Pastor Tom was quickly becoming the target of almost every group within the church. Clyde Barnes—so often depended-upon to give the pastor support—had always been the heavy-handed church boss and now became the leader of the resistance.

Pastor Tom's excitement over the new evangelism initiative faded as quickly as it had begun. On every side he was getting scorched by the heat of controversy, division, and anger. He knew he was defeated, so reluctantly he gave up his Tuesday night plans. Discouragement covered Pastor Tom like a blanket of cold snow.

QUESTIONS FOR REFLECTION

TRANSFUSION: Leading a church through change is an art form often overlooked by the passionate pastor.

1. How wisely did Pastor Tom inform his wife and the church of his heart and life change?
2. Were there other ways the church could have been prepared for the coming changes?
3. What are some ways Pastor Tom could have led change differently?
4. How should Pastor Tom have reacted to rejection and criticism?

CHAPTER FOUR

THE VISITOR

In the midst of all the backlash of the now-failed evangelism initiative, Pastor Tom kept noticing one family who returned week after week to the Sunday morning services at St. Matthew's. They were friendly enough, but very non-committal. Bill Mason, his wife Natalie, and their two daughters had checked the visitor card for six consecutive weeks. When a sizable check from Bill Mason showed up in the offering one Sunday, Pastor Tom's curiosity led him to discover that the Masons were among the few first-time guests on Easter Sunday.

On the way home from church, Tom brought up the subject of Bill and his family.

"Sandra, I wonder if the Masons are church-hopping or interested in transferring from another congregation?" His ministerial conscience told him he should call them, but somehow his good intention got snuffed out by the busyness of the week.

The Thursday after Pastor Tom had queried his wife about Bill Mason and his family, his administrative assistant Sue handed him the day's appointments. Thursday was his primary study time, so phone calls and appointments were normally off limits during the morning and slim for the rest of the day.

"Your first appointment this afternoon is with Bill Mason," Sue told him as she reviewed other items on his calendar. "He is a newcomer and would not say what he wanted. He stated only that he wanted to discuss a personal matter with you."

At exactly 1:00 p.m., Sue rang Tom's office. "Your 1:00 is here."

Bill entered Tom's office and the two men exchanged common pleasantries.

"Tell me a little about yourself," Pastor Tom said as they sat down.

For the next thirty minutes, Bill briefly told his life story to Pastor Tom. He had graduated from MIT with a MBA, but after a few years in business changed careers and took up flying. Recently, he had moved to Pleasant Valley after accepting a job as the corporate jet pilot for Armco Packing in Des Moines.

From his past experience with pastors, Bill hesitated to lead the conversation with his key question, but finally he decided that it was time.

"Well, you are probably wondering why I asked for an appointment with you," Bill began slowly but firmly. "I would like to ask you only one question. How do people in your church know how to go to heaven?"

For a split second, Pastor Tom was caught off guard. With his renewed passion to reach out to spiritually unresolved people, the question didn't really surprise him. What did surprise him was his instant awareness that he had never been asked that question before in all his years of ministry.

Do I know how to explain the answer in simple terms? Pastor Tom wondered to himself. Immediately his mind raced back to that day only a few weeks before at the lakeside cabin, where in desperation he himself had learned the answer to Bill's question. During his time spent with God that week, he had fallen on his face, begging for forgiveness from his sins. He had been flooded with peace and assurance of his genuine salvation. Yet, he was unsure how to explain what had happened to him to someone who might not understand.

As he considered the opportunity before him—and remembered the numerous times he had failed in the past with people like Larry—Pastor Tom knew he had to move forward. His heart was beating fast with anticipation as he thought to himself, *There is no better time than the present to help someone find Christ.* With that, Pastor Tom shared his personal testimony.

"A few weeks ago," Pastor Tom began, "I spent a week at a cabin on Blue Lake just to find God for myself. On the first afternoon I was there, I was reading from a daily devotional book by John Wesley when that day's reading really grabbed my attention. It penetrated my heart so much, it changed my life. Here, let me find the book and read something to you." Pastor Tom went over to his desk and fumbled around until he finally found the small paperback book entitled *Renew My Heart.*

Leafing through the pages he suddenly exclaimed, "Here it is, the reading for April 22. Let me read it for you. It begins with a scripture: 'Unless you are converted and become as little children, you will by no means enter the kingdom of heaven.' Matthew 18:3 (NKJV)"

Pastor Tom kept on reading from the words of John Wesley. "The first step towards entering into the kingdom of grace is to become as little children—lowly in heart, knowing yourselves utterly ignorant and helpless, and hanging wholly on your Father in heaven for a supply of all your wants. It is further true that unless you are turned from darkness to light, from the power of Satan to God, except you are entirely, inwardly changed, renewed in the image of God, you cannot enter into the kingdom of glory. Thus must everyone be converted in this life, or he can never enter into life eternal."

Pastor Tom put the book down on his desk and began his story.

"Bill, I have a confession to make. Until that day in late April, I had only assumed I was a Christian because I was trying to be as good as I could be. But I must say I was never what you would call truly converted. Later that day, as I read the story of John Wesley's own conversion, I found myself praying to God for the same heart and life change that Wesley wrote about. I became desperate—hungry—to have an inner assurance that I was truly part of the family of God. I needed to know deep within that Jesus had forgiven all my sins, and I was ready for Heaven. Something happened to me and I have not been the same since."

As Pastor Tom shared, Bill listened intently. Finally, as Pastor Tom paused, Bill asked, "How can I know that my sins are forgiven?"

Again, Pastor Tom had never encountered this question before in his ministry. He remembered during one of the Symposium on Evangelism seminars, the presenter had taught a simple plan of salvation with a series of Scriptures. Tom had even memorized them for future reference. As they came to mind, Pastor Tom rehearsed those verses with Bill and crudely explained salvation in Christ.

Pastor Tom's confidence and enthusiasm grew as Bill asked questions and he was able to answer them with Scripture.

Finally, Pastor Tom looked straight into the eyes of Bill and asked, "Is there any reason why you can't ask Jesus into your heart right now?"

"No," Bill replied.

Suddenly, Pastor Tom understood what ministry was all about. All the other joys of Christian service faded in comparison to hearing Bill repeat the words of a simple prayer to receive Christ. For the first time, Pastor Tom felt truly fulfilled and valued as a servant of Christ.

"This is really what it is all about," he thought to himself. "From now on, I will make leading people to Christ the focus and intention of everything I do."

After Bill prayed, the next few minutes were filled with laughing, crying, and rejoicing. Bill declared this to be the greatest feeling of his entire life. Although he was used to flying, he had never been quite as high in spirit as he was right now. He felt light as a feather. The heavy load of sin and guilt that he had carried for years was gone. He was truly forgiven.

"Say, why don't we get together again next week," suggested Bill, brimming with new enthusiasm. They decided that Starbucks would be the place.

Looking out his office window, Pastor Tom watched Bill as he walked briskly to his car. He thought to himself, *Bill is my first convert. He is the first person I have ever led to Christ.*

Tom in his excitement knew it would be hard to wait until his meeting with Bill next week, but he immediately went to work putting together some material to discuss.

THE TURNING POINT

During that first meeting at Starbucks, the two men embarked on a spiritual journey that would bind them together around a mutual purpose for the next several years.

"What brought you to St. Matthew's last Easter?" Pastor Tom asked Bill as they sat down outside in the warm morning air to drink their coffee.

"Well," started Bill, "you won't believe my story, but here it is anyway.

"My wife and I were brought up in the Orthodox Episcopal Church. We both attended church schools. I was even what they called a Worship Herald. My assignment was to walk up the aisle with a banner, which I placed at the front of the church. But not long after we were married, we drifted from the church and soon did not attend at all.

"Although we had been blessed with two beautiful children, we decided to begin the adoptive process after hearing about the orphans and need for adoptive parents for Romanian children. After battling red tape and spending thousands of dollars, we brought home a curly-headed, brown-eyed baby boy, whom we named Michael. Before he was two, our hopes and dreams for Michael crashed when we were told by the doctors that he would never fully develop mentally and would spend his entire life in a wheelchair.

"When we heard this news, we were crushed. We began asking some specific questions that led us on a quest for spiritual things. You know, questions like 'Why did this happen to us?' 'What is the meaning of life?' 'Is there a hereafter?' and 'Where will we go when we die?'

"After some discussion we decided that probably the church would be the best place to find the answers to our questions. We started visiting churches in our neighborhood. We decided we would attend for several Sundays to get the overall feel of the place. Then if we liked the church, I would set up an appointment with the pastor to ask the same question I asked you last week, 'How do people in this church know how to go to Heaven?'

"The last five years has seen our family visit fourteen different churches. Pastor Tom, St. Matthew's is the 15th church we have visited and you are the 15th pastor to hear my question. Yet, you are the first and only pastor that could give me the right answer!

"For all the others, when I asked about Heaven, they started talking about joining the church, getting active in the church, and doing good things. Not one of them said anything about how Jesus died on the cross in my place because of His great love, how to confess my sins, or how to know I am going to Heaven. Not one pastor could or did answer my question.

"Last week, after we met in your office, my life was changed. I rushed home to tell my wife Natalie about my newfound faith and joy. In fact I helped her pray to receive Christ just like you helped me. Now, we want to know what the next step is. What else should we be doing?"

Upon hearing this question, Pastor Tom began to realize how his theology needed to shift from mere theory to actual practice. The questions just kept coming. For the first time in his life he had been asked by someone how to receive Jesus as Savior, and now he was being asked how to continue to grow in Christ. Where actually should a new believer begin his spiritual journey? What should be the first step?

Pastor Tom chose his words carefully. "That is a very good question. I am so glad you have asked it. Because of my own faith journey, I cannot answer your question right away. Would you mind if I could give it some thought this week, do some research, and return next week with my answer? By the way," Tom said, "why have you never brought your adopted son Michael to church?"

Bill hung his head. "We took him with us to some of the first churches we visited, but we soon discovered people had a hard time dealing with him. He was often looked at strangely and it also affected how people treated us. In fact when we left one church Natalie said, 'Was it just me, or did those people really shun us today?'

"Anyhow, we decided to not put him through more rejection until we knew how the church felt about him. So my question for you, Pastor Tom, is this:

"Will he be loved and accepted here at St. Matthew's? Or will your people have a problem with his handicap like some of the other churches we have been to?"

"I wish I could answer that," Pastor Tom said. "I would like to say everyone will accept him, but I can't answer for the congregation. I can answer only for myself—Michael is welcome in my church and also in my home."

Pastor Tom and Bill had agreed to meet for one hour, but this first Starbucks encounter went far beyond their agreed-upon time. Both men needed to get back to their offices and work.

Pastor Tom interrupted the short silence in nervous urgency. "Bill, is there anything else I can do for you?

Bill's response was quick and precise. "Michael starts school this fall and Natalie and I are concerned that we find just the right school for his special needs."

After a short but spirited prayer, Bill returned the inquiry back to Pastor Tom. "What pressing needs do you have that

I can pray for?"

"Would you please pray with me," Pastor Tom responded quickly, "that God will raise up some men and women in this church who feel the call to reach out to hurting and spiritually unresolved people?"

Bill's prayer was simple, but encouraging. When he finished, he looked at Pastor Tom with excitement in his moist eyes. "Could I be the first to sign on with you in your mission?"

Pastor Tom spent the rest of the afternoon digging through some old files to locate long- forgotten discipleship lessons in an effort to answer Bill's question as to what was next in his spiritual journey. What he found was out of print, but seemed like the perfect material for Bill's needs. He asked Sue to make some copies, and he was ready for their next meeting at Starbucks.

SUMMER AT STARBUCKS

Week after week, Pastor Tom and Bill met at Starbucks. During each encounter, the two men would engage in dialogue concerning various items regarding faith and practice. Pastor Tom quickly realized he was also learning about how to know Christ and how to live the Christian lifestyle more than he had learned in his previous forty-four years. He liked to refer to it as being "a fully devoted follower of Christ." Seminary didn't teach him that.

Most weeks, the hour-long discipleship session would end up with a discussion about how things were going at church. Pastor Tom had been forced to step back from his demands to make Tuesdays the soul-winning night. The Ladies' Missionary Auxiliary had won back their meeting night, yet Pastor Tom refused to make an open show of how disheartened and defeated he felt. The conversations focused on church activities and strategies for future growth.

Since his career switch a few years back, Bill had often wondered how he could use his business knowledge to help others. As he talked with Pastor Tom, Bill realized his business expertise could be used to help Pastor Tom lead St. Matthew's into the future.

"Pastor Tom, I would like to make you an offer. What about us forming a partnership? I need help growing in my Christian walk. You can help me. You need help developing a plan of action for the church. I can help you. If you will continue teaching me in my faith, I will share with you what I know about leading an organization like the church on a mission. We have this system at work called Peer Mentoring. It is where two workers team up to mentor each other. What do you say?"

"It's a deal," replied Pastor Tom. "In fact, let's get our families involved also. I want to invite you, Natalie, and the kids over for a July 4th cook-out. My brother Ryan and his family are coming down from Rapid City, South Dakota. We'll have a terrific time!"

The cookout was truly a blazing success. All three families hit it off really well. The kids loved playing with each other; the men talked sports and fast cars, and the women had similar interests as well.

Pastor Tom tried constantly to turn the conversation toward spiritual matters. He knew his brother seldom attended church, and his wife Cheryl was not very religious either. He hoped his enthusiasm about his faith, combined with Bill and Natalie's, would show his brother's family how he had changed. However, Ryan and Cheryl didn't seem to notice or respond to anything spiritual.

The next morning Ryan and his family headed back north, except for their oldest son, Matt. Matt had persisted in his argument that he should be able to visit with Cousin Brent for a couple weeks.

After supper the next evening, Matt and Brent were playing catch out in the yard as Pastor Tom and Sandra watched. They enjoyed just sitting on the back patio swing together and didn't say much. That is, until Sandra spoke up.

"Tom, I really like Natalie. She and I are so much alike. We have so many common interests. I feel this could be the beginning of an amazing friendship."

A couple weeks later, Bill and Natalie returned the cookout favor by inviting Pastor Tom and Sandra over for a barbecue. With fewer kids around, Sandra began to bond with Bill and Natalie's special needs child, Michael. She noticed how much care he required and how Natalie was constantly working with him. She made up her mind what she would do to help.

When school orientation came up in August, Sandra was the first in line to volunteer for the special needs class where Michael would be enrolled. In helping him, she found herself naturally spending more time with Natalie.

Sandra and Natalie became inseparable friends. They went shopping together and often stopped for coffee on the way home. During this time of casual fellowship, spirituality and faith became the topics more and more. Sandra was growing more curious about the difference in her husband's life, and also what made Natalie so different from other women she knew.

THE PASTOR GETS A NEW WIFE

One day in early September, Natalie and Sandra had finally gotten the kids down for a nap and went into the school lunch room for a break. As usual, the conversation turned to things about God. Sandra hesitated, then blurted out, "Natalie, ever since Tom came home from his *cabin experience* I have felt like something is missing in my life. He seems to have something going on between himself and God, and I feel left out. And then since we met you and Bill, I see that you have a peace in your life that I don't have. I am beginning to wonder if I am Christian in name only. I believe in God, but I am unsure of my relationship with Him. If I died, I don't know if I would go to heaven. I am afraid all the bad things I have done would block me from getting in. I guess you can say I don't feel forgiven."

In her sweet, gentle way, Natalie spoke softly. "Sandra, don't you think it is time to ask Jesus to forgive your sins? You can invite Christ to come and live in your heart and wipe out all your sins and past failures."

By now, Sandra was sobbing. "Yes, but I don't know how I can do it."

"It is very simple," Natalie continued. "If you will repeat this simple prayer after me, Jesus will hear and answer."

Through her tears Sandra prayed, "Lord Jesus, I come to you as a sinner. I am sorry for all the wrong things I have done. Please forgive me and take me just as I am. I now receive you as my Lord and Savior. Amen"

At that moment, Sandra started her brand-new life in Christ.

QUESTIONS FOR REFLECTION

TRANSFUSION: Trying to Be a Good Person Falls Short of a Personal Relationship With Christ

1. How does a personal relationship with Christ change our view about others?
2. Do you think Pastor Tom was fully aware of how his efforts of discipleship would eventually lead to a change in the church?
3. How important is one-to-one discipleship?
4. How possible is it to be a Christian in name only?

CHAPTER FIVE

CHURCH GROW EXPO EXPLOSION

Nothing had gone as Pastor Tom expected. So many of the well-laid plans had backfired! From the very moment he had declared himself the leader of a new evangelism initiative, there had been a rising crescendo of unrest. He had dodged a chorus of bullets and had no choice but to lay low through the summer. He decided he would regroup and relaunch in the fall, if at all.

One late fall afternoon, Pastor Tom was thumbing through the most recent edition of *Preacher's Monthly* and the bold headlines of one of the advertisements caught his eye.

"ATTEND THE THIRD ANNUAL CHURCH GROW EXPO."

"If you and your church have grown weary in well-doing, then bring your key leaders and give yourselves a shot in the arm."

"Maybe this is what I have needed all along," mused Pastor Tom aloud to himself. *"I wonder who would be willing to join me for this conference."*

As he met with Bill the next week, Pastor Tom discussed the possibility and benefits of attending such a conference.

"What have we got to lose?" Bill asked. "Nothing has worked so far to turn the church around. Perhaps we will discover a new approach that will be accepted at St. Matthew's to reach the people of Pleasant Valley."

Over the next week, Pastor Tom met with every person one by one who he thought might have any desire in going to the Church Grow Expo. Some were interested, and some were not. When he finished working through his initial list, only six men committed to join him in Minneapolis.

Excitement was high on a sky-blue day in early October morning as seven guys loaded into the church mini-van and headed north to the famed Wooddale Church in Minneapolis where the Church Grow Expo was being held.

The next three days were nothing like Pastor Tom had ever experienced before, even at the Symposium for Evangelism he had attended in the spring. The atmosphere was charged with passion and enthusiasm. Every speaker had a fresh story to tell of phenomenal growth. One church had even grown from 79 to 2200 in three years! The speakers told about how they had changed their methods and fired up their people to reach out into their communities. The focus was on compassion in action before there was confrontational evangelism.

Tom and the men from St. Matthew's took copious notes. They huddled between sessions to discuss what they felt would work at St. Matthew's. With each new story of explosive growth, some grew more excited, while some were skeptical. But together they began to form a new vision for their church. Some in the group could hardly wait to go home and initiate much-needed change. One workshop especially caught Pastor Tom's attention. It was "How to Lead Your Church Through Change." Tom bought the speaker's book, *Leading Change*, and read it every chance he had. He immediately saw where he had made some bad decisions and needed to change the way he led. When Pastor Tom and his charged-up inner circle returned home, they came with a toolkit full of community outreach initiatives.

Immediately they set about making changes. One of the first changes they felt should be made was the catastrophic disbanding of the age-old choir, which seemed to be lagging although it dominated the worship landscape every Sunday and even special services.

Early the next week after the Minneapolis Church Grow Expo Conference, Pastor Tom had a discussion with Martha—the choir director—about the idea of discontinuing the choir in favor of a contemporary worship team and band. She slammed the door as she left his office quite upset, and on Friday, a signed petition showed up on his desk. It had most of the names on the roll of St. Matthew's registry on it. It was signed by members and non-members alike, many of whom Pastor Tom had never met. People were coming from out of nowhere to keep the choir at St. Matthew's.

Pastor Tom didn't know what to do. He was reliving the torture of the early spring. He did too much in response back then, so this time he did nothing. "If only they would give the new format a chance," Pastor Tom reasoned, "they will grow to appreciate it."

However, a couple of Sundays later, the front rows of the sanctuary were filled with menacing scowls. The joy of the Lord was nowhere to be found.

"Where is the pulpit?!" asked longtime member Sister Margaret. "Somebody has stolen the pulpit!"

"Where did these drums come from? Was there a rock 'n roll concert in here this week?"

That week, Martha, the choir director, had been told that all the choir seats would be removed and the choir was to sing standing on new choir risers, then leave the platform instead of sitting there all through the service. Martha's usually charming disposition turned almost evil as she led the choir. The whole atmosphere was charged with dissension. Pastor Tom only had to look at people to know the changes were not being accepted. If looks could have killed, he would have dropped dead on the spot.

As Pastor Tom stood up to speak, he could see through the glass doors of the sanctuary five of his most prominent elders huddled up close in the lobby of the church. Pastor Tom couldn't help but notice their gestures and flamboyant movements of disapproval. They were obviously not happy with how Pastor Tom was changing their treasured church.

The following week reminded Pastor Tom too much of that week in the early spring after his retreat at the cabin. But this time, the rumors and insinuations were more vicious. The removal of the choir seats and the disappearance of the pulpit were the hot button conversations throughout the church community. Tom couldn't believe that just removing the pulpit and choir seats would cause such a ruckus.

After a day of golf on Thursday, Pastor Tom returned to his office on Friday morning to find a white envelope on his desk. **TOM** in big letters was clearly printed on the front. He opened the envelope to discover a letter from Clyde Barnes, the chairman of the Board of Elders. The note was inflammatory and condemning.

"I can no longer support you and the direction you are taking the church. Accept my resignation and take my name off the membership roll. Several families are leaving St Matthew's with me and we will be transferring to another church." Just as predicted, the next several weeks saw the attendance slowly decline at St. Matthew's as several families left the church in disgust. Pastor Tom had failed once again.

IN THE VALLEY OF THE SHADOW OF DIVISON

It was the morning after the first hard freeze when Pastor Tom decided to take a brisk walk from his home to the office. He hoped the walk and the cold air would clear his mind. The falling leaves everywhere around him reminded him of the falling pieces of his dream. He wanted so much for St. Matthew's to make a difference in the community. The evangelism and church growth initiatives had seemed so right for other churches, but so wrong for St. Matthew's. He couldn't understand why they hadn't taken him to his dreams for the church. He wondered if he was the cause of the problems. Perhaps it would be best for him to resign and get out of the way. Maybe someone else could bring a fresh face to St. Matthew's and make the church effective.

When he got to the office, he pulled out his legal pad and made two columns. At the top of one column he wrote SAD and at the top of the other column he wrote GLAD. He thought about a third column named MAD, but refrained, keeping only two columns. Below each word he wrote down the names of the people in the church who would be either SAD or GLAD if he were to leave. What he saw startled him. The columns were almost even, at least according to his calculations. A majority vote could go either way. Pastor Tom made two more columns, "Reasons to Stay" and "Reasons to

Go." Again the columns were almost even.

All morning long, the confusion of recent events settled around him like a deep fog. Thoughts of resigning overshadowed everything he tried to do. He lost the power to focus. He tried to work on some reports on his desk, but couldn't because of the sickening feeling deep inside. He decided he needed to step back and rethink all of the happenings of the past year. He thought wistfully of taking another trip to the cabin by the lake. But the cabin had been recently sold and that was out of the question.

With a splintered congregation, Pastor Tom knew both he and the church were at a crossroads. Just before lunch, he reached a decision. He would seek counsel—and soon!

INDECISION TIME

Sue buzzed him at exactly three minutes to noon. "Your lunch appointment is here." With a sigh of relief, Tom shut down his computer. He probably would not come back after lunch. He had some serious thinking to do.

His lunch appointment was with Gary, the pastor of Grace Fellowship, a growing church in a neighboring town. Tom had met Gary at the Church Grow Expo and they had decided then to get together for lunch. If ever there was a right time to have lunch with a pastor who seemed to have it all together, this was the day. Tom was full of questions that demanded immediate answers.

"Hi Tom," Gary chirped cheerily.

Why does he always have to be so upbeat? thought Tom.

As he climbed into the passenger's seat of Gary's tiny

vintage sports convertible, Gary noticed Pastor Tom's dismal disposition.

"Say, brother, you look like you have just lost your best friend. What's up?"

Tom looked out the window at the gray sky and thought long before he spoke.

"You might say, Gary, I am in the valley of indecision."

During the remainder of the ride to Applebee's and all through lunch, Tom shared with Gary his recent spiritual journey—Larry's untimely death and the despair it caused in his mind and heart, the cabin conversion, the failed attempts at transforming St. Matthew's with evangelism and church growth initiatives, the painful exodus of disgruntled church members, and his deepening despair at the whole process.

When Tom had finished, Gary thought a moment in silence.

"Do you know what I didn't hear you talk about during your whole story?" Gary began warmly. "I didn't hear you say anything about what you are learning about leadership and who you are accountable to. What I did hear you say was that you have been acting like the Lone Ranger without Tonto. You have been working by yourself, trying to find your way without so much as a friend or peer coming alongside for encouragement, support, prayer, or hope. Now, you are at cross purposes with your elders and the congregation because you are dictating change instead of leading change. You are not building a team, which is one of the first things a good leader does."

Suddenly Tom remembered the workshop he had attended at the last conference and the book he had purchased. After reading only a few pages, it was left forgotten on the shelf. "How soon we forget," he mused.

"I know just what would greatly benefit you, Tom. You need to join a network of ministers who meet regularly to encourage, mentor, and sharpen one another in ministerial skills and leadership. It just so happens that I facilitate such a group each month. I'd like for you to check us out. If you like what you see, I would love to have you be a part of the group. We simply share our battles, confess our weaknesses, and celebrate our successes…all in a mutual bond of community."

For a moment, Pastor Tom recoiled at the very idea. He had never been much for confessing weakness or sharing failure. He was a proud man and the very idea of admitting defeat was repulsive. Yet, as Gary shared insights from a recent meeting, he softened to the idea. His back was against the wall and he knew something had to be done. Perhaps this was the thing he should try. Anyhow, it was better than doing nothing.

The question remained—would he be able to head off a major church split? Even his presiding bishop had expressed his fears about the future of the church and Tom's leadership there.

HUMILITY TAKES CENTER STAGE

As long as he lived, Pastor Tom would never forget that first Clergy Network Meeting. He joined with six other pastors from his and a sister denomination. As the meeting began, he was shocked at the straightforward honesty of each pastor. Every pastor was openly frank about his personal struggles, doubts, and frustrations. After each person shared, the other pastors would stop the meeting long enough to pray over him for God's grace, strength, and wisdom.

Pastor Tom was encouraged just to know he was not alone with his onslaught of emotions. Finally when the turn fell to Pastor Tom, he stumbled. He wasn't used to expressing his emotions so outwardly. Yet, it wasn't long before courage overcame his fears and he began to speak freely. Pastor Tom shared how he used to dread preaching, but had become excited to preach the Bible after his cabin experience. He told them how beaten-up he had been by the confusion, hurt, and discord over the last six months.

"Honestly, several times I have reached the point where I wonder if the ministry is worth all the hassle. In my pain, I have even thought of running and never darkening the door of the church again." The words were Pastor Tom's, but they surprised him as they came from his lips.

The mere thought of that last statement sent chills up his spine and down deep within his soul. As he spoke, Pastor Tom realized that he was doing much more than talking; he was confessing. He was confessing his fears, his doubts, his anxieties, and his mistakes. He was dropping his mask. Yet, his confession before his peers wasn't the most astounding discovery in his mind and heart. He realized he was actually humbling himself before God. As the other pastors offered their encouragement and support, Pastor Tom began to see that he had failed to surrender his dreams, hopes, and ambitions to God. He thought he had done so at the cabin, but it became clear to him that a more thorough surrender was desperately needed.

As he thought about this, he dropped his head and began to pray out loud. "Lord, I want to surrender everything… totally. But I don't know how to do it," he sobbed. If the other pastors had an answer for him, he didn't hear it. He was too busy confessing his pride before the Lord.

Immediately, he felt six pairs of hands come upon his shoulders. Prayers were prayed and tears flowed. Never before in his life had he felt such a high level of support, comraderie, and inner cleansing. Through their willingness to listen and pray for him, his fellow ministers had effectively helped Pastor Tom discover the flaws in his own leadership style and how so much had led to his present crisis.

After a brief break, Gary brought the group of pastors back together for an activity.

"Today, I want us to develop a personal timeline of our lives."

Gary gave everyone a piece of poster board and Post-it notes, with a few simple instructions. As Pastor Tom worked through his timeline, he began to uncover several cause and effect situations, punctuated by "aha!" moments in his life. He discovered that he had numerous pains and hurts in his past that led to his authoritarian leadership style.

Back in his office that day, Tom made a revolutionary decision. There should be a traditional message about gratefulness on the Sunday just before Thanksgiving. Yet, Pastor Tom chose instead to preach about "Healing the Sores of Past Hurts." The crux of the message was a second major confession to the congregation of St. Matthew's. As he prepared for the service, he recalled how his first confession—a confession that he hadn't truly been saved before his cabin retreat—didn't work so well. He wondered what damage this next confession would cause. Yet, he was determined to go forward with the knowledge and assurance that God was in control, and all he had to do was be obedient to His leading.

CHANGE POINT

In a bit of historical irony, the St. Matthew's congregation would later look back at this confession as the day the church began to change. They would remember how their pastor wept though his sermon. He had a new tenderness and brokenness they had not seen before.

As Pastor Tom shared from his personal timeline, he asked forgiveness for his heavy, dictatorial leadership style. He admitted that he had tried to force things upon the people without their understanding and hadn't waited upon God's perfect timing. That morning, Pastor Tom became "Coach Tom" and officially called a time-out.

Pastor Tom declared that the proposed time-out be focused upon prayer and seeking the full will of God. He read II Chronicles 7:14 and explained that this was the way to truly discover where and how God was working, and join Him.

At the conclusion of the message, Pastor Tom asked for people to join him at the front of the church for prayer. He knelt down and was joined by twenty others from the congregation. The prayer time seemed awkward—with no outward emotion shown—but the awkwardness became the catalyst for change. That morning the heart of St Matthew's Church began to change! More important, Pastor Tom's heart began to change.

QUESTIONS FOR REFLECTION

TRANSFUSON: Facing Sins and Past Failures With Humility Will Bring Lasting Change

1. What did Pastor Tom do differently when attending the second conference?
2. Is it possible to bring about change too quickly?
3. How differently should Pastor Tom have handled the changes that needed to occur?
4. How hard is it to be humble?

CHAPTER SIX

PUTTING PRAYER FRONT AND CENTER

It was a sunny, chilly Iowa winter Monday morning with a skiff of fresh snow. Pastor Tom looked out his office window and reflected on the transforming time of prayer at the front of the sanctuary the day before. He was reminded of the fourth discipleship lesson he and Bill had discussed last summer at Starbucks. Its title was "How to Pray." At the time, Pastor Tom did a great job emphasizing the importance of prayer, yet no ongoing prayer plan had been implemented. As he reflected further, Tom remembered the day when he stopped by the church on his way to go golfing. Even now he could still remember the twinge of guilt at his attitude of resentment. It had started when Steve Crenshaw confronted him in the church parking lot with a color brochure for an upcoming prayer conference. He realized at this point that he needed to swallow his pride and call Steve.

"Hey Steve, last spring you gave me a brochure about a prayer retreat happening in Des Moines. I admit, I tossed the brochure long ago, but it seems like the date was in December of this year. Are you planning on going? If so, I would like to join you. I would like to bring Bill Mason along as well."

Pastor Tom could only imagine the look of shock that had to have come over Steve's face as he heard his pastor's voice on the phone. Not only was Pastor Tom voluntarily calling him, but he was asking to attend a prayer retreat with him. Steve was surprised and amazed.

Once Steve got over his initial shock, excitement replaced the surprise in his voice.

"Of course, Pastor. That would be great. In fact, you and Bill don't need to worry about a thing. I will make the reservations for you and Bill, myself."

The week passed quickly and it was the day of the Back to Prayer conference. Pastor Tom and Bill jumped into that familiar black sedan he had avoided on so many occasions. What a sense of humor God must have. Tom was actually enjoying the ride!

Together, the three men drove to the mega Grace Church in downtown Des Moines. As they listened and participated, they were drawn into the power of what God was doing through the national prayer movement. It seemed God was moving mightily around the world in answer to the focused prayers of His people.

"What would happen if the people of St. Matthew's began praying like that?" The question seemed to pervade the discussion on the trip home. "Would God work on their behalf like He has done so many places around the world?"

As the three men arrived at the church and separated to their own vehicles, they decided together that they would attempt to be the catalyst for the prayer movement at St. Matthew's. They agreed to get together once a week and ask God to work a miracle in their church.

Pastor Tom knew what was first on his agenda. At the conference he had attended a seminar on The Pastor's Prayer Partners. He would gather five or six men into his office before the Sunday morning service and have them pray for him and the worship service.

DISASTERS THAT KEEP ON HURTING

L ater when Pastor Tom returned to his office, he glanced at his calendar. January 21st, the 25th anniversary cel-ebration of St. Matthew's, was just around the corner. In discussing this church milestone with his Clergy Network Group, he had decided to dig through the history of the church for interesting insights into her history. When Pastor Tom rummaged through the dusty church archives, he discovered that St. Matthew's had been started as a daughter church of a downtown Des Moines church—Grace Church—in fact the very church where he had just attended the Back to Prayer conference.

When it came to selecting a name for the new church, several people had ideas, but dear old Aunt Bessie's idea prevailed. She wanted it to be named St. Matthew's as a reminder of the church's call to the Great Commission in Matthew 28:19. After all Aunt Bessie was a charter member of Grace Church and became one of the founding members of St. Matthews.

Pastor Tom soon discovered that the first three years of St. Matthew's history saw phenomenal growth, but the growth was short-lived due to an internal power struggle. The fledging church, which seemed to have such a bright future, was found spiraling downward in crises after the founding pastor was forced to resign because of mismanagement of funds. Several who supported him left in disgust, some even returning to the mother church in Des Moines.

The families who left were the ones who were financially influential, leaving the immediate future of St. Matthew's in question. But soon the church had rallied and continued to grow when another struggling church group agreed to merge with her. This incoming group was led by a strong layman, Clyde Barnes.

After the merger, the new incoming leadership brought St. Matthew's out of immediate doom and into a period of recovery. During this time, a good-sized youth group was formed. For these youth, missions was their focus. They loved helping and serving people. One of their favorite summer activities was a week-long trip to the Native American Indian Reservations of North Dakota. Even though some of the parents hesitated sending their children so far away, the spiritual benefits seemed to outweigh their fears until one fateful summer day.

The events recorded during the ninth year of the church's history riveted Tom's attention. That summer, the youth group was returning from their annual mission trip when their church bus was hit head-on by a pick-up truck heading the wrong way on the interstate. The bus burst into flames and eighteen people lost their lives—fourteen were under the age of twenty-one. The driver of the truck was driving drunk; it was recorded as the worst drunk-driving accident in US history.

The drunk driver survived the crash and was convicted of multiple accounts of manslaughter, assault, wanton endangerment, and DUI. He maintained that he remembered nothing of the accident and was sentenced to sixteen years in prison. After eleven years, he was released from prison because of good behavior. He moved in with his parents not far from the scene of the accident. Several people at St. Matthew's were so enraged that he would be released early that they even drove up to the Hamilton County courthouse to testify against his early release.

This disaster dealt a crushing blow to the congregation—

not only for the loss of eighteen lives along with the decline in attendance, but for the pain and sorrow of those left behind. The grieving process went on for months. When the driver was released early, the unresolved grief turned into frustration, despair, and anger as members allowed their emotions to overcome them, leading to continual criticism of each other. Finally the youth pastor resigned in frustration.

Several months after the release of the drunk driver, a significant rift occurred in St. Matthew's. For years, divergent theological views were simmering between key leaders and finally brought to a boil, aggravated by the ongoing pain and grief felt by all. An ugly confrontation occurred, which resulted in 60% of the congregation leaving to form a new congregation.

Over the years, Clyde—the strong layman from the merging church years before—strengthened his role as influencer and was elected as the Chairman of the Board of Elders.

His tenure proved to be a true roller-coaster ride, with good years followed by bad years. Each of the bad years turned into another reason for a new pastor, resulting in five pastors over fifteen years. One pastor had an affair with a member of the choir. He was forced to leave town in disgrace, while the choir member stayed on at St. Matthew's with no public apology. For years, there had been contention over what seemed to be inconsistent and unfair judgment.

Two pastors had left after short tenures to take other, more successful churches. One pastor discovered that ministry was not right for him and he took a job as a semi driver. Pastor Tom's predecessor was there only two years, but he had been a stabilizing influence, and attendance at St. Matthew's had improved slightly.

When Pastor Tom came to Pleasant Valley, he and Sandra committed to St. Matthew's because of a growing positive attitude the people seemed to have toward the future. On the surface, things appeared to have gotten better. They talked a good talk, but somehow the conversations always seemed to revert to their past struggles. Sometimes, it would be reminiscing over "the glory days," when everything was going well and the attendance was up. But mostly, it was about the pain and suffering felt down through the years. So often, people played the blame game, seldom taking responsibility for what happened to them. It was always "the bishop should have done things differently," or "that pastor did it wrong," or "this person caused the problems." If they couldn't find someone to blame, they would ask, "What if?" Some of the things had occurred years ago in St. Matthew's history, yet they continually came up in conversation.

HEALING THE HEART OF THE CHURCH

One day it hit Pastor Tom like a ton of bricks—it would be impossible for this church to move forward until God brought healing for past hurts. He thought about the incredible pain the church had been through—but more than that, he thought about the personal pain each individual had suffered. Then he realized that corporate hurts are often based on personal injuries.

Pastor Tom knew he had to begin a deeper spiritual journey himself in order to help his people personally discover healing from past hurts. So along with planning for the 25th anniversary of the church, he began to plan another and far more important meeting.

On the last Sunday of December, Pastor Tom announced to the congregation that he was calling a very special meeting of the entire church to be held in two weeks, on Friday evening and Saturday morning. It was called the *"Where We Have Been, And Where Are We Going?"* **meeting.**

When curiosity caused a good number of people to gather on Friday evening, Pastor Tom told them about how he had developed a personal timeline at his pastors' network meeting and how he had gained new insight and release from his own past pain. He asked the people to sit around tables in groups of eight to ten and develop their own personal timeline, and then share it with others at the table. Some were reluctant at first but then people really began to get into the exercise and the meeting went on for nearly three hours. They started to see how charting the timeline of their life helped them begin to identify and deal with the past hurts of their lives. Pastor Tom tried to show them how past baggage affects and contributes to who you are and how you act and react to others. When they concluded with prayer, you could hear sobs throughout the room.

As they gathered on Saturday morning, Pastor Tom led them to move from a personal timeline to building a church timeline. They put on the wall the list of significant events that had shaped the life of the church. Here is a list of some of what they came up with—

- The different power struggles within the church
- The mistreating and firing of the founding pastor
- The tragedy of the mission team kids being killed by a drunk driver
- The group who had merged with a different agenda

and theology
- The pastor who had an affair with one of the ladies in the choir
- The pastor whom everyone liked had left in mid-year.

It was as if God showed them that the heart of the church was wounded. When they had finished with that process, Pastor Tom led the church in a prayer of confession to God. They confessed the wrongs they had done personally. They confessed the wrongs of the church. The result was absolutely amazing. Once the old hurts were confessed and dealt with, a new atmosphere prevailed. People who had been estranged from one another asked each other for forgiveness and wept together. As the spirit of prayer and worship pervaded throughout the church family, God began to heal their hurts and disappointments. A new spiritual energy filled the room as they began to think about the upcoming anniversary in a new light. This should be a starting line, not a finish line. The 25th Anniversary Celebration of St. Matthew's became known as the Rebirth of St. Matthew's Church.

THE BAPTISM

During the past year, Pastor Tom had learned so much. His head was still spinning from his own heart and life change, and seeing the church come back from the brink of major division. Just days before an inevitable split threatened the very existence of the church, the 25th Anniversary Celebration had become a spiritual and numerical success by all accounts. Even though people kept celebrating the benefits of the BIG DAY, Pastor Tom knew it would take more than one outstanding service to bring St. Matthew's full circle so they were effectively reaching people outside the church. With all his past efforts at evangelism, however well-intentioned (though misdirected), there was still something missing. A new emptiness began to haunt him. He began to realize that so much of his evangelism energy had been forced. There was a lack of spiritual power. A new hunger grew in his soul. He found himself spending more and more time in prayer. He also found himself reading everything he could find about great evangelists and evangelism.

ONE LIFE-CHANGING STORY

One day Pastor Tom began reading the story of Dwight L. Moody, one of America's great evangelists, of whom it was said that one million people came to Christ under his ministry. As he read, he was awestruck and deeply convicted. This is the story he read:

"In 1869 while working with the YMCA in Chicago, Dwight L. Moody went with his wife to England to discover the secret of evangelism. Sitting on a park bench in London, the well-known evangelist Henry Varley told Moody, 'The world has yet to see what God will do with and for and through and in and by the man who is fully consecrated to Him.' Those words burned into the heart of Moody. He returned to Chicago with a great desire to build the largest Sunday School and church in the city and soon took pride in having the largest Sunday night congregation in Chicago. However, there were few conversions, which made him realize more and more how ill-prepared he was for this great work. Moody continued to hunger for a deepening of his own spiritual life and experience even though it appeared on the surface that he was being greatly used by God.

"In the fall of 1871, he kept noticing two women who attended his meetings sitting on the front row. He could see by their expression that they were praying during his message. At the close of the service one night, one of the ladies came up to Mr. Moody after he felt he had preached very well. He expected her to compliment him on his success, but instead she said,

" 'We are praying for you.'

" 'Why don't you pray for the sinners who are present,' Moody replied. 'I am all right.'

" 'You are not all right because you don't have the power,' she replied.

" 'I need power?' Moody exclaimed! 'Why, I thought I had the power!'

"From then on, Moody was belligerent toward those dreadful women when they were present and miserably lonely when they didn't come. However, after two months an intense hunger and thirst for spiritual power were aroused in him and he began to have a desire for what they were praying. He did not know what it was, but he began to cry out to God as never before. Moody really felt that he did not want to live if he could not have this power for service.

"On Friday night, October 6, 1871 Mr. Moody asked the two ladies to come and talk with him. As they poured out their hearts in prayer for him that he might receive the Holy Spirit. Moody also prayed, begging God,

" 'Lord, baptize me with the Holy Spirit and fire.' Two nights later on October 8, 1871, the great Chicago fire burned his church to the ground. He never saw many of his congregation again.

"Mr. Moody went to New York City to collect funds for the victims of the Chicago fire, but his heart was not in the work of fundraising, because he was crying out to God all the time that He would fill him with His Spirit and baptize him with power from on high.

"Then one day--'O what a day it was!' Moody exclaimed later, as he was walking down Wall Street--God answered his prayer for the baptism of the Holy Spirit, and the power of the Spirit fell upon him. He quickly hurried to the home of a friend and asked for a room. He stayed in the room for hours alone with God as the Holy Spirit flooded his soul with a joy he could not describe— almost too sacred to talk about. He had such an experience of His Love that he had to ask God to stay His hand. When he returned to Chicago and began preaching again, the sermons were no different, yet hundreds were converted. He declared he never wanted to go back like he was before."

As Pastor Tom read the account about Moody, he began to realize what the missing piece was. Now he knew what was missing in his life. His eyes filled with tears and he began to sob,

"O God, do it again! What you gave to Dwight L. Moody, please give to me. I need the infilling of the Holy Spirit." He dropped his head on his desk and the hunger of his soul became unquenchable.

Tom lost any sense of time as he prayed on and on, but he knew he would not leave that room until he had received an answer from God. Like Jacob in the Bible who wrestled with the angel, Tom declared, "I will not let You go, God, until You fill me with your Holy Spirit." He slipped out of his chair onto his knees. He surrendered all his burdens: his grief over his parents' death; he surrendered his wife and his children; he surrendered the people of St. Matthew's Church; he surrendered his past accomplishments and future ambitions. As he surrendered, he could feel a new sense of release from bondage. His relentless prayer of faith reached the heart of God. All heaven came down! The baptism had come!

QUESTIONS FOR REFLECTION

TRANSFUSION: Spiritual Preparation Is Absolutely Essential For a Pastor and Church to Become Healthy Enough to Reach Out Into the Community.

1. What was Pastor Tom willing to do to turn a negative situation into a positive situation?
2. How much does a church's past affect its present and its future?
3. What part does prayer play in church health and growth?
4. Is "being filled with the Holy Spirit" optional or essential?

CHAPTER SEVEN

WHAT A DIFFERENCE A YEAR MAKES

It was a great day to be alive! Pastor Tom's cell phone rang early.

"Are you ready to swing those irons on the golf course today?" It was Bill's chipper voice, shining into his ear.

"Yes, sir! Meet me in half an hour at the church," replied Pastor Tom.

As they traveled north, Tom couldn't help but remember how he felt driving alone on the same road a year earlier and how differently he felt today. For a few brief moments his mind raced through several of the life-changing events that began on that traumatic day.

"Hmm," Tom mused out loud. "What a change a year makes! Bill, have you noticed that ever since our 25th Anniversary Celebration, there has been a new excitement at St. Matthew's?"

"Yes," replied Bill. "I have noticed that many of the old members are taking on new life. People who have been only Sunday-morning attendees are signing up for extra Bible studies, and there is a new excitement about serving. And, Pastor, I have also noticed the change in you! Your sermons get better every Sunday. You have a new anointing and a new confidence. Did you see the crowd that came forward last Sunday praying to be filled with the Holy Spirit?"

With excitement Tom replied, "That was a powerful service, wasn't it? Have you also noticed how new visitors are impressed with the church and some keep coming back?"

"The best thing that has happened," Bill exclaimed, "was cleaning out the old baptismal that hadn't been used in years. I am so glad I was one of the first group of five baptized in that 'Renewing the Baptism' service. And now when people pray to receive Christ, we just might use that baptismal on a regular basis."

"And another thing that is making a great difference," Pastor Tom added, "is the pastor's prayer partners that gather to pray for me before each service. Everyone can see the results when the prayer warriors pray."

"Tom," prodded Bill after a brief pause, "what are we going to do to keep the momentum going in the church? The last few weeks have been the best. But it doesn't seem like we have a purpose or plan on what to do next."

"Well, Bill," declared Tom, "you are exactly right! I believe it is time to discuss what our next step should be. What do you say that we spend some time today talking about a new chapter of vision and mission? Would you agree the place to begin is to hammer out some kind of a Missional purpose plan, based on whom God has called and designed us to be as a church?"

"I do agree!" Bill nodded emphatically.

All during the rest of the drive to the Bedford Green Golf Course, Pastor Tom and Bill engaged in an energized conversation about what the true vision and mission of St. Matthew's Church could or should be. There was never any debate about whether or not to adopt a Missional plan, the question was what should it be, and how would it be accomplished.

A NEW BEGINNING

Soon Bill and Tom were back on the same golf course where Tom had received the fateful phone call the year before. In between plays, they talked about how the church should become more Missional in everything it did. They were energized by the big picture of what could happen if people in the church would catch a fresh vision. Leaving the 7th hole, Bill exclaimed, "Pastor, what if you would choose some key influencers in the church who would make up a Missional leadership team? You could meet with them regularly to develop a new strategy. That would give consensus to the changes that need to be made."

Pastor Tom readily agreed and immediately began to think about a "team leadership" and of various people in the church who might serve on such a team.

Reaching the 8th hole, Bill hesitated and then reluctantly spoke as if thinking out loud. "You know, Pastor, there is something that has always bothered me."

"What's that, Bill?" replied the pastor.

"Why is it so hard to get people involved in serving at the church?" stuttered Bill.

"Mmm," mused Tom. "Maybe it is because they have never been taught about serving."

They golfed on before the conversation could be resumed. Walking back to the club house after completing all nine holes, the conversation centered on the ongoing struggle of how to get people to want to volunteer. Finally Tom spoke almost as if thinking out loud.

"I could begin with a sermon series on spiritual gifts, which would spark the people's interest in how they could use their passion and strengths to help fulfil the mission. A study on individual gifting would show how each person could be uniquely equipped for a specific ministry."

Tom went on to suggest that this kind of study could actually be the basis for people with similar giftings to be grouped into teams.

"Hey," cried Bill, "we could call this new strategy, TEAM-UP, which would stand for Together Experiencing A Ministry= Unlimited Potential!

Seated at a table in the clubhouse, they soon boiled all of their ideas down to four main themes. Tom scribbled on a napkin: 1. Prayer; 2. Building relationships; 3. Receiving Christ; and 4. Discipleship. The next question was about how to make these themes into teams. Pastor Tom raised the idea of a series of sermons about how important teams are to the health of the church, focusing on each of the four themes. All during the drive home, their discussion centered on how to implement these new concepts. Both men returned home relaxed, but anxious to move forward.

A NEW STRATEGY TAKES SHAPE

When Tom was finally back in his office the next day, he pulled out a legal pad and began to write down some names to contact for a Missional Leadership Impact Team. He looked at each person's passion, gifting, and availability. Finally he had four people in mind.

Debbie had a passion for prayer
Joe was always engaged in some compassion-in-action
project
Andy loved to share the gospel with people one-on-one
Tim was a great mentor and disciplemaker

One by one, Pastor Tom met with the people on his list and found that each one affirmed his choice. Debbie chose the prayer theme; Joe wanted to focus on outreach projects; Andy declared his passion for seeing people come to faith in Christ, and Tim was all for discipleship.

Later that week Pastor Tom was excited to bring all four people together along with Bill to brainstorm how to launch this new concept of TEAM-UP so it could be an effective tool to reach their community for Christ. After much discussion, a timeline for the launch of TEAM-UP filled the wall marker board. It would be called the "Dream Summit Weekend." It looked something like this:

Timeline for the DREAM SUMMIT WEEKEND:

Weekend Preparation	= Saturday Afternoon	= Saturday Night Summit	= Sunday Morning Summit
Recruit team leaders	Meet with team	Food/teaching	Message of recruitment
Have ministry fair	Leaders plan/pray	Teams pray together	Team sign-ups

Timeline for FOLLOW-UP AFTER
the DREAM SUMMIT WEEKEND:

Next Saturday Follow-up Meeting	Forward Progress
1. Have meeting the following Saturday	1. Monthly team Leader meetings
2. Four teams establish goals	2. Continual evaluation of team ministries

It was 11:30 that night before the meeting finally broke up after an intense session of prayer. Everyone was passionate about what they believed God was leading them to do.

THE SERMON SERIES THAT CHANGED EVERYTHING

The next big question; how to begin to change the heart of the church so they would be willing to be led in a new direction? As Pastor Tom prayed, he was impressed to think about two sermon series. Well, really one series with two parts. He would begin with a series on how God has gifted each believer with certain passions and skills, and then follow with another series of messages on Team Ministry. TEAM=Together Experiencing A Ministry.

DREAMS TO TEAMS FAIR

Through the ups and downs of the past year, Pastor Tom had come to understand how communication and momentum are essential ingredients in congregational life change. On the last Sunday of the sermon series on spiritual gifts, Pastor Tom lost no time in announcing that reaching the lost and spiritually unresolved should be a whole-church affair. Woven into his message, he explained how he believed each person was uniquely gifted by God to reach others for Christ. Immediately after the three messages on how God has gifted each believer, Pastor Tom launched into the second part of his sermon series with the focus on team ministry, suggesting four teams. Having met with the team captains several times, they had suggested having a "Dreams to Teams Fair." They decided to hang four colorful banners in the worship center depicting the four teams of outreach, and their themes.....

***THE A TEAM** Advance Prayer Warriors*

***THE B TEAM** Bridge Builders Brigade*

***THE C TEAM** Conversion Coaches*

***THE D TEAM** Discipleship Trainers*

A Dreams to Teams Fair was prominently set up in the fellowship hall. Each of the four captains set up a table representing their respective field of ministry. As Pastor Tom preached the message each Sunday about a Bible character that best represented one of the four areas of outreach, he invited people to visit the tables and pick up materials. The fifth message was to conclude the Dream Summit Weekend and ask for sign-ups.

BLAST-OFF

Scores of people showed up to participate in the Dream Summit Weekend. Following the Saturday night event, several stayed around, going into the church sanctuary to pray. After a time of kneeling around the altar for prayer, someone suggested that they go throughout the worship center and lay hands on every seat, praying for those who would come to worship. The next morning Pastor Tom's message was about joining a team to make a difference. At the close of the message, he invited everyone to go to the fellowship hall, and he encouraged them to select the team they were most interested in and to sign on. The service was actually concluded in the fellowship hall with each team captain praying with his new team! And so, after much prayer and planning on the concluding day of the sermon series with the message on *"How to Give Our Church Away,"* TEAM-UP was officially launched at St. Matthew's on the first Sunday of May.

QUESTIONS FOR REFLECTION

TRANSFUSION: Lasting Change Depends on a Well-Crafted and Well-Executed Strategy.

1. What was the reason for the new spirit of optimism?
2. What is the best way to approach and bring about a new vision and mission for the church?
3. Was the congregation involved enough in setting the new direction for the church?
4. How would you have developed a strategy for change?

CHAPTER EIGHT

THE STORIES BEGIN

A few weeks earlier as Pastor Tom was concluding his teaching on the A Team (Advance Prayer Warriors), he had challenged the congregation to pray for the meanest person in town. What if God could save the worst? Then no one else would have any excuse.

Debbie, the captain of the A Team, was given the names of Sam and Eva Tadlock who ran a sheep ranch south of town. Sam was known in the area for his heavy drinking and unprovoked fighting. Some had even referred to him as the meanest man in town. Eva had been in church as a teenager, but after marrying Sam, she had adapted to his sinful lifestyle. Sam was a rough-and-ready gun-toting Texan who hated churches and preachers. The Advance Prayer Warriors put Sam and Eva on the prayer list and began to pray for their salvation.

One day Joe, captain of the B Team learned from a neighbor how the Tadlocks had lost a number of their prize sheep to a pack of wild dogs, resulting in a severe financial loss. Since Joe had also been handed their names as two people the prayer team was praying for, he and his wife went by to visit and talk with Eva about what they could do to help. She was openly embarrassed about the condition of their land and buildings, not even wanting to invite them into her house. When Joe offered to get some people together and spend a day helping fix things up around the place, Eva knew that Sam would resent anybody coming on his land to work. Finally Eva agreed to let some people from the Bridge-Builders Compassion Team from St. Matthew's come one Saturday when Sam was out of town and do some odd chores and repairs.

When Sam returned the next day after the Compassion in Action Work Team had been there, he couldn't believe his eyes. Why would anyone do all that work and expect nothing in return? Then he learned that over the past six weeks, his wife had been secretly attending St. Matthew's Church when he was either drunk or gone. His first response was anger, which soon melted into curiosity. The next Sunday, he decided to drop his wife off at St. Matthews. He wouldn't attend church himself, but he wanted to get a glimpse of this unusual church.

As Eva got out of her husband's big cab-over Ford sheep truck and started toward the church, Pastor Tom was standing on the front porch of the church. When he saw Sam staring at him through the open cab window, he walked out and said, "Hi, Sam. That's one of the best- looking trucks I have ever seen." Immediately Sam, bursting with pride, got down and began to show Pastor Tom some of the features of his prize truck.

Abruptly, after a few minutes of truck talk, Sam said he was very busy and had to go. As Pastor Tom walked toward the church he threw a backward glance and was surprised to see Sam still standing there looking at him. Pastor Tom said, "Sam, why don't you come to hear me preach sometime?"

Sam shouted back, "I'll be here next Sunday." And so he was! In just a few weeks Sam came sobbing to the altar and became the first convert of St. Matthew's new renewal season. The first thing Sam wanted to do was to be baptized in *"that there water tank."* The transfusion had begun!

A PASTOR IN DISTRESS

As Pastor Tom drove to his office with his windows down, he couldn't help but be energized by the wonderful smells of a late-spring morning. This was a great season of ministry. Over and over again during recent weeks new people had visited the church, and many had found new life in Christ. What a spiritual thaw, compared to the years of spiritual frozen wasteland! As he pulled into the parking lot, his cell phone rang. His administrative assistant was on the line telling him that Pastor Jim Benton of the Cedar Creek Church had called and sounded quite upset. Could Tom meet with him for lunch? Lately, meeting with pastors in distress was becoming a new part of Pastor Tom's ministry. He was quickly learning that pastors everywhere were discouraged and facing the same struggles both personally and in their churches that Tom had faced so many times.

WARNING SIGNS

The next morning Tom's wife, Sandra, looked at him with a troubled glance as they sat at the table eating breakfast. "Tom, you look so pale; are you feeling well? I noticed that you spent very little time in the bed last night." Because of his difficulty in breathing, Tom had to sleep some nights in his big lounge chair in the den.

Tom laid the morning paper down and eyed his wife meekly. "You always were able to read me. No, I am not feeling well. Maybe I should see my doctor for a check-up. But I am so busy with all the new frenzy at church that I feel like I am being run over by a fast train."

"Honey," persisted his wife, "please make an appointment with your doctor!"

THE FIERY FIVE

One day at the beginning of summer, Pastor Tom was in prayer when he was reminded of the Great Apostle Paul's words in Acts 20:24. "But my life is worth nothing to me unless I use it for finishing the work assigned me by the Lord Jesus—the work of telling others the Good News about the wonderful grace of God." (NLT) As Tom continued to think and pray, it suddenly dawned on him.

"I should be mentoring and equipping next-generation leaders in what it means to be fully committed and Missional in all areas of life and ministry." So Pastor Tom went on a searching mission. Before long, he had recruited five young ministerial students from the nearby Berea Bible College. They had jumped at the opportunity to sign on for a one-year residency intern program at St. Matthew's Church. The opportunity dovetailed with their school's requirements for graduation. In addition to serving in various roles, they agreed to be mentored by Pastor Tom in his new idea of TEAM-UP evangelism. Tom was in uncharted waters, creating a residency program, but decided it was so necessary that he would just wing it.

Pastor Tom met with his new staff weekly as a group, and also spent time mentoring each one individually. He soon found his days beginning to grow longer and more intense, but so many exciting things were happening that he continued to push himself more and more, to the point of exhaustion.

QUESTIONS FOR REFLECTION

TRANSFUSION: Stories of Life Change Are the Greatest Test of a Church's Change of Heart.

1. What impact did the stories of life change have on the church's momentum?
2. Why did Pastor Tom overlook the warning signs of his marginal health?
3. How important was the recruiting of resident interns to help with the ministry?
4. Could Pastor Tom have accomplished the same purpose by not developing leaders?

CHAPTER NINE

THE UNEXPECTED AND UNTHINKABLE HAPPENS

Crash! Bang! Thud! Tom's administrative assistant, Sue heard the unmistakable sounds coming from Pastor Tom's office. Then all was silent.

"What was that?" shouted a couple of the resident interns who were walking down the hall. Everyone rushed to Pastor Tom's office and hesitated a moment before bursting through the door. There beside his desk on the floor lay the crumpled form of an unconscious Pastor Tom. One of the resident interns immediately called 911. Soon the scream of sirens had whisked the limp pastor away.

"Where am I?" Tom asked with slurred speech as he slowly regained consciousness.

The blurry white figure bending over him said softly, "You are in the ICU unit on the 3rd floor of New Haven Regional Medical Center." Gradually, Tom had a foggy flashback. Wasn't this the same area where he had come to see his friend Larry and found that he had already passed away? He began to remember the sinking feeling of meeting the distraught family in the hallway just outside the ICU.

Soon there was a flurry of medical personnel performing multiple tests. Finally the verdict was in. The stroke on Tom's left side had left him unable to speak clearly or to walk without assistance.

AN UNLIKELY PLACE FOR A STAFF MEETING

T wo weeks had passed by when the phone rang in the office of St. Matthew's Church. It was Pastor Tom, asking to speak with his administrative assistant.

"Pastor, how are you doing?" Sue asked, surprised to hear his weak voice with some words still slurred.

"Better today," Tom replied. "In fact, I have just come back from physical therapy. I am learning to walk all over again and have done some speech exercises." He continued, "Say, I would like for you to have my staff and the resident interns come to the hospital for a staff meeting."

"A what?" Sue replied, noticeably shocked.

LESSONS LEARNED FROM A HOSPITAL BED

S t. Matthew's pastoral staff and the five resident interns ventured slowly and apprehensively into the pastor's hospital room at the New Haven Regional Medical Center. Pastor Tom was sitting in a chair beside his bed, greeting them warmly.

After chatting for a while, Tom began: "I want to thank you all for coming. There are a few things I need to share with you. I have been learning some valuable lessons that may change the way we all do ministry. I think I would like to call them

"God's handwriting on the ceiling: Lessons I learned from a hospital bed."

For the next hour they talked, laughed, and planned

together as Pastor Tom shared some of the things God was teaching him, such as:

God's ways are not always our ways.

Lone Rangers don't build God's Kingdom.

It's not so much what God does through us as what He does to us.

"Oh, I am sure God has many more lessons to teach me, but I am taking one day at a time and doing a lot of listening and reading," said Pastor Tom.

THE SONG MUST GO ON

When the lesson was finished, Pastor Tom spoke openly to the five resident interns in the room. "I have to share some news with you. The doctor says that I will need to take at least a six-month sabbatical to go through rehabilitation and regain my strength. So, what does that mean for St. Matthew's Church and your ministry there? I would like to ask each of you to stay on an additional year and begin to assume a greater role in ministry and responsibility."

"There is some other unfinished business," continued Pastor Tom. "We have launched a new evangelism strategy called TEAM-UP, but the area that is most lacking is some discipleship material. Could you guys write something that would be meaningful to our new converts? And to think of it, there are no written guidelines for the other three teams, either. Would you guys like to work up some good ideas for TEAM-UP?"

All of the resident interns nodded a strong assent in unison. After prayer the meeting was concluded and goodbyes were said. Those leaving the room that day had a new sense of calling and responsibility.

THE FIRST ORDER OF BUSINESS

Pastor Tom had asked Glenn to act as the leader of the group of resident interns. Upon returning to the church, he immediately brought everyone into his office to discuss how they could carry on in the pastor's absence. It was agreed that he would meet with the pastor once or twice a week, as he was able, so they could keep him updated on their progress.

"What about Pastor Tom's request that we develop some discipleship material?" asked Neil, one of the other resident interns.

"Good question," Glenn responded and immediately asked which team in the TEAM-UP strategy each resident intern would like to work with. Neil spoke up with excitement. "Give me the discipleship team." The other resident interns each chose a team, and soon more assignments were made. Neil already had a general idea of how he was going to proceed, and the others followed his example.

When Neil left the meeting, he made an appointment with Tim, the captain of the D Discipleship Team. Tim and his team soon gathered and were overjoyed to think about having a resident intern work with them. They immediately accepted Neil's offer to write some discipleship lessons. He came up with three booklets. They consisted of three levels of discipleship, beginning with entry level on up to more mature lessons.

Personal Bible Study: (3 lessons) to be used in one-to-one discipleship.

Setting Sail: New Life Adventure Part 1: (7 lessons) to be used in group discipleship.

Climbing Mountains: New Life Adventure Part 2: (7 lessons) also group discipleship.

When the booklets were finally finished, Tim's D Team all agreed that someone on the team would personally meet and greet each new convert and give them the first booklet, *My Personal Bible Study Book*. They would offer to spend an hour with them, going over the material.

Neil then suggested that he and Tim, the D Team captain, could find a good teacher/facilitator and invite all the recent new converts to come together for a group study using the material *New Life Adventure, Setting Sail* to be followed by the additional material, *New Life Adventure, Climbing Mountains*.

After the first class session, Neil shared with the other resident interns that he had found his sweet spot and was going to fully dedicate all his time and energy to the area of discipleship. Each of the other resident interns chimed in chorus that they too had found the area that fueled their passion.

Over the next few months, as Pastor Tom was able, he mentored the young resident interns. He declared later that it was interacting with these five bright young ministerial students that motivated him and helped in his recovery. St. Matthew's enjoyed the favor of God as multitudes came to faith in Christ. Baptisms became a pleasant routine. As the congregation of St. Matthew's grew in love and service, the community of Pleasant Valley was impacted far beyond anyone's wildest dreams. And Pastor Tom continued to learn valuable leadership lessons as his health slowly but surely returned.

QUESTIONS FOR REFLECTION

TRANSFUSION: The Unexpected Often Changes the Best of Plans.

1. How could the disaster of Pastor Tom's stroke been prevented?
2. Up to the incident, were the resident interns being used to their fullest capacity?
3. Why did Pastor Tom continue to try to run the church during his sabbatical?
4. Did the resident interns help or hinder the church in the pastor's absence?

CONCLUSION

Although what you have just read is a fictional story, some of the incidents have been gleaned and adapted from the real-life stories of a number of different people I have met and known during my lifetime. Other stories in the parable show what could, should, or should not have happened. Although Pastor Tom Bachman's story is not my story, Sam and Eva Tadlock were real people. They were my very first converts in my first church, which I reopened during my senior year in Bible College. The church had been closed for forty-four years. During my three years there, over 100 people prayed to receive Christ. Maybe in your own personal journey you have identified with some parts of Pastor Tom's story. It is my prayer that you will take whatever steps are necessary to have your own spiritual transfusion.

The rest of the book contains a number of resource and implementation items that have already been used successfully in many different churches. May God bless you as you begin your own journey of ***transfusion***!

DISCIPLESHIP BOOKLETS

The three discipleship booklets printed in full here have been used in many churches to disciple new and renewing believers. You are free to use in any way that serves you well. You may also download them from the www.teamupevangelism.com website and copy them for your use.

My Personal Bible Study Book

Basic Bible Studies for New & Renewing Christians

Daniel E. Finch

My Personal
Bible Study Book

Table Of Contents

Where Should I Begin? 2

Suggested Devotional 3

The Bookcase of the 66 Books of the Bible 4

My Personal Bible Study 5

    Lesson 1. How to Walk in Christ 5

With Confidence
With Courage
With Commitment

    Lesson 2. How to Live in Christ 9

With Community
With Conviction
With Compassion

    Lesson 3. How to Grow in Christ 13

With Prayer
With Bible Study
With Ministry

Where Should I Begin?

Are you wondering how you can ever learn all you need to know about the Bible? Do all those different books, chapters and verses seem like a mountain too big to climb?

What you have in your hand is a "Do It Yourself Bible Study."

It is so simple that all you need is a Bible to get started.

Sit down, read and mark the following pages. Your Great Adventure to understanding God's Word has just begun.

DO NOT DEPEND UPON FEELINGS

There will be times very early and even throughout your Christian life that you will not feel like you did when you first accepted Christ. In those times you must learn how to live by faith. That means you will trust God and His Word—not your feelings to be the assurance of salvation.

The train diagram below illustrates the relationship between FACT (God and His Word), FAITH (Our trust in God and His Word, and FEELING, (the result of our faith and obedience, John 14:21)

The train will run with or without the caboose. However, it would be useless to attempt to pull the train by the caboose. In the same way, we, as Christians, do not depend on feelings or emotions, but we place our faith (trust) in the trustworthiness of God and the promises of His Word.

Are you ready to begin your spiritual journey?

Suggested Devotional For New Christians

It is important to begin the habit of listening and talking to God each day. Bible reading helps us to know who God is and how we might grow in our relationship with Him.

TO HAVE PRODUCTIVE BIBLE STUDY:

1. PRAY TO UNDERSTAND THE SCRIPTURE: As you open your Bible, ask God to prepare your heart and mind. . .
2. READ TO RECEIVE TRUTH: Allow your mind to be open to what God Is really trying to say. . .
3. PERSONALIZE TO DAILY LIVING: Discover how the Scripture impacts our everyday life.
4. APPLY TO EXPERIENCE GROWTH: Realize that no growth occurs until application is made. Prepare for change.
5. MEMORIZE TO RETAIN KNOWLEDGE: True growth is maintained by the memorization of scripture.

WHILE READING, TRY THE FOLLOWING:

1. Look for a verse that stands out to you personally.
2. Mark that verse with "FV" which stands for Favorite Verse.
3. Meditate on how and why this verse is your favorite.
4. Apply that verse to your daily life or use it in your prayer time. From your first scripture reading in Mark 1:1-12, verse 5, you might pray something like this: (for yourself) "Thank You for Your faithfulness, God, to forgive my sin. Is there anything I need to confess?" (Pause. If there is, God will bring it to mind.) I confess my sin of _____. "Thank You for forgiving me." (For others) "I pray for _____that they might begin to understand Your loving forgiveness as I am beginning to learn."

<table>
<thead>
<tr><th>READ</th><th>FAVORITE VERSE</th></tr>
</thead>
<tbody>
<tr><td>Day 1 - Mark 1:1-12</td><td>_____</td></tr>
<tr><td>Day 2 - Mark 1:14-27</td><td>_____</td></tr>
<tr><td>Day 3 - Mark 1:29-43</td><td>_____</td></tr>
<tr><td>Day 4 - Mark 2:1-12</td><td>_____</td></tr>
<tr><td>Day 5 - Mark 2:13-27</td><td>_____</td></tr>
</tbody>
</table>

Day 6 - continue reading through the book of Mark

        After Mark, read the Book of John

        After John, read Philippians

        After Philippians, read Acts

        After Acts, read Romans

The Bookcase of
The 66 Books of the Bible

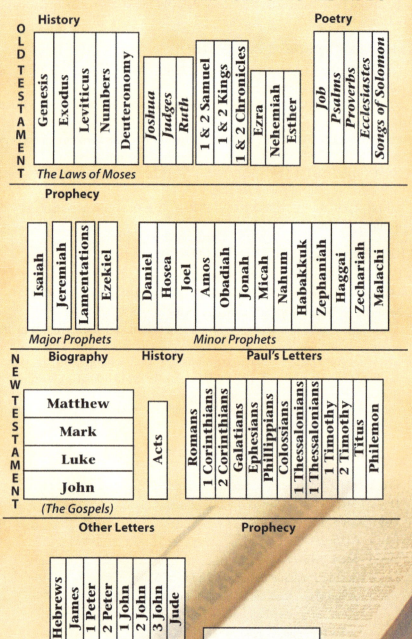

OLD TESTAMENT

History

Genesis, Exodus, Leviticus, Numbers, Deuteronomy — *The Laws of Moses*

Joshua, Judges, Ruth

1 & 2 Samuel, 1 & 2 Kings, 1 & 2 Chronicles

Ezra, Nehemiah, Esther

Poetry

Job, Psalms, Proverbs, Ecclesiastes, Songs of Solomon

Prophecy

Isaiah, Jeremiah, Lamentations, Ezekiel — *Major Prophets*

Daniel, Hosea, Joel, Amos, Obadiah, Jonah, Micah, Nahum, Habakkuk, Zephaniah, Haggai, Zechariah, Malachi — *Minor Prophets*

NEW TESTAMENT

Biography

Matthew, Mark, Luke, John — *(The Gospels)*

History

Acts

Paul's Letters

Romans, 1 Corinthians, 2 Corinthians, Galatians, Ephesians, Phillippians, Colossians, 1 Thessalonians, 1 Thessalonians, 1 Timothy, 2 Timothy, Titus, Philemon

Other Letters

Hebrews, James, 1 Peter, 2 Peter, 1 John, 2 John, 3 John, Jude

Prophecy

Revelation

How to Walk in Christ

*"Be An Upstream Christian
In A Downstream World"*
Many begin the Christian Walk
Some fail to keep going.....Why?
Takes more than talk to make a walk.

lesson_one

THINK ABOUT IT: Now that I have decided to live the
Christian life, what new challenges do I face?

Your decision to begin or renew your journey of faith will be tested. That is why it is very important to spend time studying the Bible. This lesson will help you begin your spiritual walk.

I. I NEED CONFIDENCE TO WALK IN CHRIST

A. Assurance that I am a child of God on the way to heaven

MULTIPLE CHOICE: All answers are correct, but underline only the answer that corresponds with the scripture reference.

1. Acts 3:19 tells us that we must: (1) live as the Bible says; (2) go to church; (3) accept Christ; (4) Repent or turn to God and give up our sins.

2. John 3:16 teaches us that those who receive eternal life must FIRST: (1) confess their sins; (2) live a good moral life; (3) believe, have faith in Christ; (4) pay their tithe.

3. I John 1:9 states that our sins are forgiven if we: (1) Ask Christ to forgive us; (2) confess our sins to God; (3) are sorry we have sinned; (4) believe that we should stop sinning.

4. John 1:12 is a wonderful promise that states: (1) ask and you will receive; (2) Christ can perform miracles; (3) by putting our faith in Christ, we have the right to become His children; (4) God always keeps His word

5. Revelation 3:20 reveals that before we accept Christ, He is (1) interested in us; (2) speaking to us; (3) wanting to help us; (4) seeking to enter our life by knocking at our heart's door.

B. Assurance that I am loved even when I sin:

TRUE OR FALSE

_____1. Christ has great patience with those who have sinned
                                                      -I Timothy 1:15-16

_____2. Jesus fully understands our weaknesses and helps us in time of
        Need   -Hebrews 4:15-16.

_____3. Jesus refuses to help the believer who sins   -1 John 2:1

THINK ABOUT IT:
How is Christ beginning to help me change my lifestyle?

II. I NEED COURAGE TO WALK IN CHRIST
Taking the first steps is both difficult and exciting

A. Courage to begin my new walk in Christ
MATCH UP the scripture reference with the correct statement

1. Revelation.3:20   _____ A. The Bible was written to help you have faith in
                                  Christ and know that you have eternal life.

2. John 3:16   _____ B. When we accept Christ, we become a new per-
                                  son, the past is gone, everything is new.

3.1 John 5:11   _____ C. You will be saved if you believe in Christ and
                                  acknowledge Him as Lord.

4. II Corinthians 5:17   _____ D. If we have God's Son, we have eternal life.

5.1 John 5:12   _____ E. God gives us eternal life which comes from God
                                  to us through His Son, Jesus

6. Romans 10:9   _____ F. Christ knocks at the door of our life and If we
                                  will open o Him, He will come in.

7.1 John 5:13   _____ G. God loves us so much that He gives us His Son;
                                  and accepting Him we have eternal life.

From these verses, how do you know that you are a Christian?

_____

B. Courage to face my everyday world.
FILL IN THE BLANK

1. F_____ in Christ is the V_____ that over-
   comes the world.   -I John 5:4

2. The God who lives in _____ is greater than the One who
   lives in the W_____.   -1 John 4:4

3. The best way to overcome temptation is to r_____ the devil.
                                                              -I Peter 5:8,9

THINK ABOUT IT:
How do others recognize my NEW LIFE IN CHRIST?

III. I NEED COMMITMENT TO WALK IN CHRIST

"It usually takes at least "3" weeks for one to feel comfortable in performing a new
practice. And it takes about "3" more weeks to make the practice a part of oneself.
But many new Christians don't have the commitment to continue for "3" days."
                                                              -Dr Jay Adams

A. Getting the will-power to walk in Christ
GIVE A SHORT ANSWER

1. What may we receive by asking God?   -James 1:5

2. When Christ provides the strength, what are we able to do? -Philippians 4:13

3. What is a good way to exercise self-Control?   -Titus 2:11-12

B. Finding the time to develop my new walk in Christ

1. Matthew 6:33 -Learn how to Rearrange my priorities

2. Ephesians 5:16- Learn how to Redeem the t _____

3. Ephesians 4:23 - Learn how to Renew my m _____

THINK ABOUT IT:
What will it cost me to be fully committed to Christ?

T.A.W.G. DEVOTIONS	SUMMARY AND
Time Alone With God	APPLICATION

Beginning My Walk

Day 1: Keep walking with Christ
Colossians 2:6 _____

Day 2: Think like a new person
II Corinthians 5:17 _____

Day 3: Live a NEW LIFE
Romans 6:4 _____

Day 4: Fellowship with other Believers
I John 1:7 _____

Day 5: Live a lifestyle of love
II John 6 _____

Day 6:Do right things to others
Ephesians 2:10 _____

Day 7: Follow the example of Christ
I John 2:6 _____

LOOKING AHEAD TO LESSON 2

How to Live in Christ - Through Community
Through Convictions
Through Compassion

How to Live in Christ

lesson_two

Some Christians look like Christ
Others look like everything but.....
Most of us are off and on............

*"... Just as you received Christ Jesus as Lord,
continue to live in Him ..." -Col. 2:6 (NIV)*

THINK ABOUT IT:
Having chosen to become a follower of Christ
how should my life compare with His life?

Every person who receives Christ will soon sense a desire to live a lifestyle pleasing to God. There will also be a desire to share with others how God is changing thoughts and actions. Most of the time people are more impressed with how we live than what we say. In this lesson, we will study how others can begin to see more of Christ in us.

I. I NEED COMMUNITY WITH FELLOW BELIEVERS

• Through public worship each week.
• Through group Bible study.
• Through involvement in ministry to others.

COMPLETE THE SENTENCE

1. In I Peter 2:2 we find that as newborn babies want milk, so as new Christians we should crave _____.

2. In Hebrews 10:25, Paul told the Christians to not stay away from church but to _____.

3. Once each week, Jesus would always go to the _____ according to Luke 4:16.

TRUE OR FALSE

_____1. According to Acts 13:1-3, Barnabas did not cooperate with other Believers in the church at Antioch.

_____2. Acts 1:8 shows us that true believers tell others about Jesus everywhere they can.

_____3. Ephesians 2:21-22 shows us that the church is not a building, but believers who allow the Holy Spirit to live within.

MATCH the correct statement with the proper scriptural reference. Read and study these principles.

_____1. I Timothy 3:15   A. Whoever is joined to Christ will produce much fruit.

_____2. John 15:5   B. The Church of the living God is the foundation of truth

_____3. I John 4:7   C. A church that praises God will have the favor of the community and the Lord and will add new believers to them daily.

_____4. Acts 2:47   D. If we have received New Life from Christ, we will love each other.

THINK ABOUT IT:
What is my attitude about meeting with other believers?

II. I NEED CONVICTIONS THAT ARE SCRIPTURAL

A conviction is something that you believe in without any hesitation or reservation. Sometimes there are things that the Bible does not specify as being right or wrong. They may be habits or activities. As a new believer, you may be unfamiliar with all the Biblical Commands. In the following verses, you will find principles for dealing with the questionable things in your life. MATCH the correct statements with the proper scriptural reference. Read and study these principles.

_____1. I Cor. 6:12   A. Is it a good example? Could it cause someone to stumble? (If so, I should not do it).

_____2. I Cor. 8:13   B. Is it enslaving? Does it control me? (If so, I should not do it)

_____3. I Cor. 10:31   C. Is it good for me? Does it help me grow spiritually? (If not, I should not do it)

_____4. I Cor. 10:23   D. Is it pleasing to God? Does it glorify God? (If not, I should not do it).

Search the scriptures to discover how to live the Christian Life. Biblical principles are the only safe guide to measure behavior. Reading and applying the Bible to every part of everyday life will cause you to grow spiritually. Use the following scriptures when making life choices.

APPLY these 12 scriptural tests to thoughts, words, and actions:

1. The PURITY Test -1 Cor. 6:19
   Can I do this to the body where Christ dwells?
2. The PARTICIPATION Test -1 John 2:15-16
   By doing this, will I take my eyes off Jesus?
3. The POLITE Test - Romans 14:7,21
   How will doing this affect others?
4. The PARTNER Test - Col. 3:17
   Could I invite Christ to do this with me?
5. The PUBLIC Test - I Thess. 5:22
   Will doing this give the appearance of wrong doing?
6. The PRESENCE Test -1 John 2:28
   Would I be ashamed to be found doing this upon Christ's return?
7. The PROBLEM Test - Heb. 12:1
   Will this hinder my New Life in Christ?
8. The PROOF Test - Romans 12:9
   Does doing this improve my capacity to hate evil and love good?
9. The PROCLAMATION Test - Philippians 2:15
   Will doing this void my witness for Christ?
10. The PEACE Test - Philippians 4:6-7
    After praying about it, can I do it and have peace?
11. The PASSION Test - Mark 12:29
    Will this keep me from loving God as I should?
12. The PRIORITY Test - Matthew 6:33
    Will this keep me from putting God first in my life?

THINK ABOUT IT: Where does my life need to change?

III. I NEED COMPASSION FOR OTHERS

"Sharing with others begins with caring for others. People do not care how much you know until they know how much you care." - John Maxwell

MULTIPLE CHOICE: Underline the correct answer according to the listed scripture. This will show you how the early Christians shared their faith.

1. In Acts 3:1-8 we find Peter and John sharing Jesus with: (1) their neighbors; (2) a poor cripple; (3) the disciples; (4) all the people in the temple.

2. Acts 8:27-35 records Philip talking about Jesus to: (1) the people in Samaria; (2) the king; (3) an unknown traveler; (4) a good friend of his,

3. Acts 26:1-16 is the account of Paul giving his personal testimony to: (1) a king; (2) a businessman; (3) a good friend; (4) his neighbors.

4. John 1:40-42 tells how Andrew brought his: (1) boss; (2) parents; 3) brother; (4) enemy; to Christ.

5. Acts 5:42 shows how the early believers were continually telling others that Jesus was the true Messiah: (1) in Bible Conferences; (2) in crusades; (3) in the temple and in their homes; (4) by the sea.

TRUE OR FALSE

_____1. Paul wrote in Romans 12:4-5 that Believers not only belong to Christ but to other believers as well.

_____2. Jesus told the man in Mark 5:19 to go home and not tell anyone what had happened to him.

_____3. In Matthew 28:19-20 Jesus gave clear instructions that Believers should go only to the people who want to hear and not worry about everyone else.

FILL IN THE BLANKS and discover how to share your testimony with others.

1. Letting your l_____ shine means backing up your words with a lifestyle that is genuine.   Matthew 5:16

2. Learn how to a_____ those who ask about your faith.
                                                                I Peter 3:15

3. Discover how to overcome f_____when sharing with others.
                                                                Acts 18:9-10

4. Always follow the leading of the Holy S_____.   Acts 10:19

5. The Key to successfully impacting others is found in Acts 1:8:
   "You will receive p_____when the Holy Spirit comes upon you and then you will_____.

_____

THINK ABOUT IT: List at least two people in your life (family, friends, co-workers), that you will tell about your new relationship with Christ. _____ _____

_____

TAWG DEVOTIONS	SUMMARY AND
Time Alone With God	APPLICATION
HOW TO LIVE	

Day 1 Live by the S _____
                                    Gal. 5:16
Day 2 Live by L _____
                                    Eph. 5:2
Day 3 Live W _____
                                    Eph. 4:1
Day 4 Live to P _____ God
                                    I Thess. 4:1
Day 5 Live to K_____ God
                                    Col. 1:10
Day 6 Live W _____
                                    Eph 5:15
Day 7 Live in H_____
                                    I Peter 3:8

LOOKING AHEAD TO LESSON 3: How To Grow - Through Prayer, Bible Study and Service To Others

How to Grow in Christ

Some Christians Grow Fast...
Others Grow Slow ...
Some Just Don't Grow!

lesson_three

THINK ABOUT IT: How do I want to grow?

The Bible compares the new believer to a new baby with complete instructions for the "New Babe in Christ" to GROW UP.

"Grow up into Him (Christ) in alt things." Eph. 4; 15

This lesson will help you discover three ways to grow and mature in Christ.

I. I NEED TO GROW THROUGH PRAYER - "Prayer is not overcoming God's reluctance, but it is taking hold of His eagerness."

PURPOSES OF PRAYER: All answers are correct, but only underline the one which corresponds with the scripture reference.

1. The purpose of prayer in John 16:24 is: (1) that we can share with God; (2) that we will put things in God's hands; (3) that God's will can be done; (4) that our joy may be full and complete,

2. What did Christ tell His disciples to do in order to resist temptation in Matthew 26:41? (1) Go to church; (2) Pay your tithe; (3) Stay alert, watch and pray that you won't be tempted; (4) Stay away from any place where there might be temptations to sin.

3. James 5:16 says that a righteous man's prayers are: (1) heard by God; (2) powerful and very effective; (3) sincere and earnest; (4) much needed.

POINTERS FOR PERSONAL PRAYER - What guidelines do these verses give us concerning our prayers?

1. Phil. 4:6 _____

2. Matt. 6:7 _____

3. Matt. 21:22 _____

PONDERING ABOUT PRAYER

1. What is the result when we talk to God about everything? Phil 4:7

_____

2. What is the major cause of unanswered prayer? Psalms 66:18

_____

3. Who does God hear? John 9:31

_____

_____

THINK ABOUT IT: What can I pray about specifically this week?
(personal need, damaged relationships, unsaved friends)

_____

_____

II. I NEED TO GROW THROUGH BIBLE STUDY

God's Word is the revelation of Who God is. The key to knowing God is regular Bible Study.

FILL IN THE BLANKS and learn how to study the Bible.

1. Rom. 15:4 tells us that learning the scripture gives us _____

_____

2. II Tim 3:16 tells us that all scripture comes from _____
and is good and useful to _____

_____

3. 1 Peter 1:25 assures us that the _____ of the Lord will last

_____

MULTIPLE CHOICE: All answers are correct, but only underline the answer that corresponds with the scripture reference.

1. John 20:31 shows the Bible was written so that: (1) we could know what God expects from us; (2) we may believe in Christ and find life in His name; (3) we could read and study it; (4) God might reveal Himself to us.

2. II Peter 1:21 informs us that the Gospel did not come by the will of man, but: (1) from prophets of God; (2) written by holy men; (3) men of God spoke as they were guided and moved by the Holy Spirit; (4) men who were given revelations from God.

3. In John 15:3 we find that as we read and obey the Bible, it: (1) encourages us; (2) lifts us; (3) cleanses us; (4) instructs us.

PRODUCTIVE BIBLE STUDY

1. PRAY TO UNDERSTAND THE SCRIPTURE
     Prayer prepares the heart.

2. READ TO RECEIVE THE TRUTH
     Reading broadens the vision.

3. APPLY TO EXPERIENCE GROWTH
     Application produces the change.

4. MEMORIZE TO RETAIN KNOWLEDGE.
     Memorization conserves the effort.

THINK ABOUT IT: How does Bible study change my life?

III. I NEED TO GROW THROUGH MINISTRY TO OTHERS

One of the greatest joys of being a Christian is to watch God use us and produce spiritual fruit through us.

Definition of a servant: Someone who sees a need and assumes personal responsibility to meet that need.

PREREQUISITES FOR USEFUL SERVICE - Fill in the blanks and discover how you can be used by God.

1. Matt. 22:37-39 tells us that there are two things we must do if we are to be effective in useful service: a._____ b._____

2. Find two things we are urged to do in Rom. 12:1-2:
     (Vs.1) _____
     (Vs.2) _____

3. What is the prerequisite of having a great ministry for God?   I Cor. 13

PARTICIPATING IN USEFUL SERVICE

1. According to I Peter 2:9, what do all believers (both clergy and laymen) share in common?_____

2. According to I Pet 4:10, to whom has God given spiritual gifts and how are they to be used?_____

3. When God is allowed to work in our lives what will be the results?
     Phil 2:13 _____

PERSISTENCE IN OUR SERVICE.

1. In I Cor. 15:58, Paul admits that ministry is challenging and never ending. What motivates us to continue? _____

2. Heb. 6:10-12 tells us both what to do and what not to do. Explain _____
   _____

3. What promise does God give to those who serve Him? John 12:26
   _____

THINK ABOUT IT: How can I discover my spiritual gifts?

Summary and Application

SUGGESTED STRUCTURE FOR A 30 MINUTE T.A.W.G
(Time Alone With God)

5 Minutes......Scripture Reading

5 Minutes......Write Down Insights and Application

5 Minutes......Adoration and Praise

5 Minutes......Confession and Surrender

5 Minutes......Thanksgiving

5 Minutes.....Supplication — Praying For Others and Self

30 Minutes of Intimate Communion With Christ

LIST SEVERAL WAYS TO PUT THIS LESSON INTO PRACTICE

LOOKING AHEAD: Complete NEW LIFE ADVENTURE
          Ask about One-to-One Timothy Lessons

New Life
Adventure

A Group Bible Study for
New and Renewing Believers

Daniel E. Finch

Are you new to the Christian Faith?

Do you want to Learn more about the Bible?

Welcome to your *New Life Adventure — Setting Sail!* Your life has been changed by the most important decision anyone could ever make. Both how you live now and where you will live forever have been dramatically affected by this choice.

Let this Bible Study Booklet serve as your growth guide to your new life in Christ as you connect with other believers in a small group Bible Study.

Discover how your Life in Christ is different from your life outside of Christ and how you can grow in seven ways:

1. A New Confidence 5
How To Know You Are Saved -- I John 5:10-13

2. A New Communication 9
How To Talk To God -- Luke 11:1-13

3. A New Guidebook 13
How To Understand The Bible -- II Timothy 3:14-17

4. A New Freedom 17
How To Be Forgiven -- I John 1:5-10

5. A New Challenge 21
How To Effectively Handle Temptation -- I Corinthians 10:1-13

6. A New Direction 25
How To Make Right Decisions -- Romans 12:1,2

7. A New Behavior 29
How To Improve Relationships -- John 13:21-38

*"Grow in grace and
knowledge of our
Lord Jesus Christ"*
2 Peter 3:16

"BEHOLD ALL THINGS ARE BECOME NEW." II Corinthians 5:17

Congratulations

You are now part of a wonderful adventure - THE NEW LIFE! At last you have found an eternal friend, Jesus Christ. The NEW LIFE you have in Him is described in the Bible in a variety of ways. You are now a "NEW CREATION," with a "NEW Mind," a "NEW HEART," and a "NEW LIFE." The Bible also portrays the Believer as one who was dead in sin, but brought back to LIFE. You are ALIVE unto God.

The simplest and most beautiful description of what has happened to you is where Jesus compares your NEW LIFE to being "Born." Seeing a child born is exciting. It is dramatic, unique, and yet it is only the beginning. Jesus says we are "BORN again" when He comes into our lives. Your new commitment to Him has made you a NEW person. And like the baby, you must grow and mature. Babies are not born running or talking, nor do they have a college degree. They must learn to walk, talk, grow, and develop. That is the excitement of living.

The Christian life is very similar. Think of yourself as a NEW PERSON, a baby just beginning to grow. Say to yourself, "I am growing, I am learning, I am discovering. I am searching." As you do these things, you will grow, and GROW, AND GROW.

I Peter 2:2 says, "Like newborn babies, crave pure spiritual milk, so that by it you may grow up in your salvation, now that you have tasted that the LORD is good."

There are many opportunities for spiritual growth. One of the best places to learn about the Christian Life is the NEW LIFE ADVENTURE group study. Here you will discover how your NEW LIFE IN CHRIST is manifested and the ways your life will change.

Ephesians 4:22 says, "You were taught with regard to your former way of life, to put off your old self. ... To be made NEW in the attitude of your minds, and to put on the NEW self, created to be like God in true righteousness and holiness.

BIBLE STUDY GUIDE

WHY STUDY THE BIBLE?
    Because God reveals Himself through His Word

THE BIBLE IS
    A ROAD MAP – to show us the way
    A LOVE LETTER – to express God's love for us
    A SEED – to help us reproduce God in others
    A SWORD – to war against the forces of evil

"The Bible is the source for our complete equipment to effectively serve the LORD."

God has some goals for each of us. He wants us to change, to grow, to mature and to affect others. The best way for all this to happen is through BIBLE STUDY.

These five methods of Scripture intake help you get a firm grasp on God's Word

Hear	*Romans 10:17*
Read	*Revelation 1:3*
Study	*Acts 17:11*
Memorize	*Psalm 119:9-11*
Meditate	*Psalm1:2-3*

HERE ARE SOME TIPS . . .

1. Read prayerfully
2. Read with an open mind
3. Read with pen and marker. Underline or mark important words
   Write ideas/summary on Bible Study Page
4. Read to apply to all areas of life

BE ON THE LOOKOUT FOR . . .

1. Keywords
2. Repeated words
3. Strong action words
4. Advice/warnings
5. Progression of ideas
6. Commands
7. Promises I John 5:10-13

The Bookcase of The 66 Books of the Bible

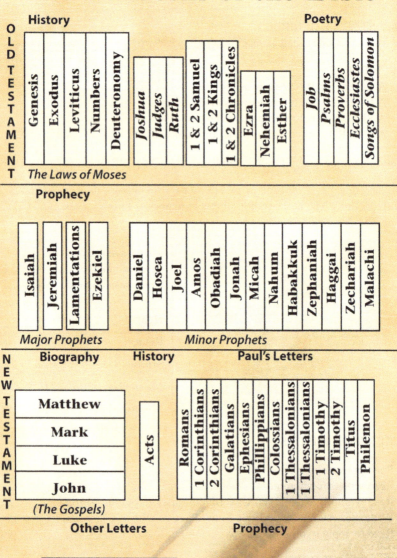

OLD TESTAMENT

History

| Genesis | Exodus | Leviticus | Numbers | Deuteronomy |

The Laws of Moses

Joshua | Judges | Ruth

1 & 2 Samuel | 1 & 2 Kings | 1 & 2 Chronicles

Ezra | Nehemiah | Esther

Poetry

Job | Psalms | Proverbs | Ecclesiastes | Songs of Solomon

Prophecy

Isaiah | Jeremiah | Lamentations | Ezekiel

Major Prophets

Daniel | Hosea | Joel | Amos | Obadiah | Jonah | Micah | Nahum | Habakkuk | Zephaniah | Haggai | Zechariah | Malachi

Minor Prophets

NEW TESTAMENT

Biography

Matthew

Mark

Luke

John

(The Gospels)

History

Acts

Paul's Letters

Romans | 1 Corinthians | 2 Corinthians | Galatians | Ephesians | Phillippians | Colossians | 1 Thessalonians | 1 Thessalonians | 1 Timothy | 2 Timothy | Titus | Philemon

Other Letters

Hebrews | James | 1 Peter | 2 Peter | 1 John | 2 John | 3 John | Jude

Prophecy

Revelation

A NEW CONFIDENCE

How To Know You Are Saved

> *MEMORY VERSE -- 1 John 5:13*

Often it is easy for a new Christian to not "feel saved." Assurance of salvation is the opposite of doubting and is based on scriptural facts. It is possible for us to doubt our salvation and not live up to the privileges God has for us.

WHAT ARE SOME REASONS WHY WE DOUBT OUR SALVATION?

_____

_____

_____

_____

_____

COMPARE THE OLD LIFE WITH THE NEW LIFE:

The Old Life:	The New Life:
1. Fear of dying	1. Peace With God
2. Uncertainty	2. Assurance
3.	3.
4.	4.

A promise is only as good as the character of the one who makes it. When we recognize the complete trustworthiness of God, the promises He makes to us are validated. For our assurance of salvation, we need only to take God at His Word. In this lesson we will study how to know we have eternal life.

I. ASSURANCE OF SALVATION COMES BECAUSE WE HAVE CHRIST IN OUR HEART

1. According to 1 John 5:11-12

   A. Who is the only source of eternal life? _____

   B. Who gives eternal life? _____

   C. Who has eternal life?_____

2. According to Revelations 3:20 what does Christ promise to do? _____ __
   _____

   A. How does Christ enter a person's life?_____

   B. Where is Christ right now in relation to the believer? _____
   _____

II. ASSURANCE OF SALVATION IS NOT BASED ON FEELINGS.

Feelings Vary, But Faith in Christ Brings Assurance — Acts 16:31

The train will run with or without the caboose. But the caboose can never pull the train. As Christians we place our faith in Christ, not our feelings.

1. When do we 'feel' like doubting our salvation? _____
   _____

2. If we trust our feelings rather than God and His Word how will this affect our attitudes and actions?_____
   _____

3. What does unbelief cause us to do? Hebrews 3:12 _____

_____

4. What is one way to deal with doubt? Hebrews 3:13 _____

_____

5. If we put our trust in God despite how we feel, how does this change our attitudes and actions? _____

_____

III. ASSURANCE OF SALVATION COMES FROM THE WITNESS OF GOD'S WORD.

1. According to I John 5:13, what reason does John give for writing this book?

_____

_____

2. According to John 20:31 what is the greatest thing that happens to us when we believe in Christ? _____

_____

3. What do all these promises from God's Word have in common?
   John 3:16; Acts 16:31; Romans 10:9 _____

_____

CHALLENGE: FOLLOW ABRAHAM'S EXAMPLE   Genesis 22

1. Expect testing, Genesis 22:1

2. Go back to God's Word, Genesis 22:2

3. Choose again to believe it, despite how you feel, Genesis 22:8

4. Continue in obedience, Genesis 22:9

QUESTION: IF YOU WERE TO DIE TONIGHT, ARE YOU SURE THAT YOU WOULD BE IN HEAVEN WITH GOD? WHY or WHY NOT?

APPLICATION: Write down the names of two people that you will share with this week why you are assured of your salvation: _____

_____

_____

FOR FURTHER STUDY:

1. When did God first promise eternal life? Titus 1.2 _____

_____

2. Why has God chosen to make our salvation dependent on His grace and not on our works? Ephesians 2:8,9 _____

_____

3. Our assurance of salvation is based on God's faithfulness. Look up the following references and discover what God is faithful to do:

   A. Deuteronomy 7:9 _____

   B. I Corinthians 1:9 _____

   C. I Corinthians 10:13 _____

   D. I Thessalonians 5:23,24 _____

   E. II Timothy 2:13 _____

4. What are some things that you see about faith in Hebrews 11:6? _____

_____

5. Suppose after you explained the grace and love of Christ to a friend, he said, "Great! That means I can sin whenever I want to, and God will forgive me." What are some of the things that you would tell your friend based on Hebrews 12:5-11 and I John 2:4?

CONCLUSION:

1. Assurance does not come if we live in the past.
2. Assurance does not come if we doubt.
3. Assurance will not come if we depend on feelings.
4. Assurance comes when we realize that eternal life begins the moment we trust Christ for our salvation. John 5:24

A NEW COMMUNICATION

How To Talk To God

MEMORY VERSE -- John 16:24

For any relationship to become meaningful, there must be constant communication. Prayer is the only way we can communicate with Christ. When a person becomes a Christian he discovers the opportunities that prayer offers.

SINCE PRAYER IS TALKING TO GOD, WHAT ASPECTS OF GOOD COMMUNICATION ARE NECESSARY? _____
_____
_____
_____
_____

COMPARE THE OLD LIFE WITH THE NEW LIFE:

The Old Life:
1. Using God's name in disrespect
2. Praying in emergencies
3.
4.

The New Life:
1. Talking to God in Love
2. Desire to pray everyday
3.
4.

Prayer is not only asking what we wish of God but offering what He wishes of us. Even though some praying comes naturally to a new Christian, we still must learn the discipline of effective praying. In this lesson we will see how prayer is the way we build a meaningful and intimate relationship with Jesus Christ.

"Prayer is best learned when we are faced with something bigger than ourselves."
— *John Maxwell*

I. EFFECTIVE PRAYING IS BASED UPON OUR RELATIONSHIP WITH CHRIST.

1. According to James 5:16, what kind of person prays effectively? _____
   _____

2. According to Hebrews 4:15-16, how can we have the confidence to draw near to God? _____

3. According to John 14:13-14, what one thing must we do before God will work in our behalf? _____

To ask in His name means to ask in His authority and on His merit.

II. EFFECTIVE PRAYING CAN BE HINDERED BY IMPROPER CONDUCT.

1. What reason for not receiving an answer to our prayers do we find in James 4:3? _____

2. If we have unconfessed sin in our lives, what does Psalm 66:18 say will happen to our prayers? _____

3. According to Matthew 6:14-15 what must we do to receive forgiveness from God? _____

4. What does James 1:6-7 say will keep us from receiving anything from the Lord? _____

III. EFFECTIVE PRAYING IS DETERMINED BY CERTAIN CONDITIONS.

1. When we pray, how does God respond? Jeremiah 33:3_____
   _____

2. What happens when people pray together? Matthew 18:19 _____
   _____

3. What limits what God does? Ephesians 3:20_____
   _____

4. In what ways does Matthew 7:9-11 tell us that God's response to our prayers is like that of a good father's response to his children?_____
   _____

5. What does I Peter 5:7 encourage us to do during prayer? _____
   _____

CHALLENGE: FOLLOW DANIEL'S EXAMPLE   Daniel 6 & 9

1. Why was Daniel unwilling to stop praying 6:10? _____
_____

2. What ingredients are a part of Daniel's prayer?

   a) Daniel 9:4 _____

   b) Daniel 9:5 _____

   c) Daniel 9:18 _____

QUESTION: ARE YOUR PRAYERS PRAYED WITH FAITH?   Mark 11:24
_____

APPLICATION: Write out a prayer to God which includes: Adoration, Confession, Thanksgiving & Supplication

   A _____
   C _____
   T _____
   S _____

FOR FURTHER STUDY:

1. What characterizes the leper's prayer in Mark 1:40_____
_____

2. Read Philippians 4:6-7.

   a) What is the wrong reaction to have toward difficult circumstances?_____
_____

   b) What is the right response?_____

   c) What is the result of this right response?_____

3. How do you think God would respond to a request for something He knew would be bad for you?

   Psalm 106:15 _____

4. In Luke 11:1-13 Jesus showed us how we should pray. List those things:

a) _____

b) _____

c) _____

d) _____

e) _____

f) _____

5. Study Passages on Prayer

    a) Luke 18:1-8   Parable of the Widow
    b) Luke 18:9-12   Parable of the Pharisee
    c) Luke 18:13-14   Parable of the Publican
    d) Luke 11:5-13   Parable of the Friend at Midnight
    e) Matthew 18:23-35   Parable of the Unmerciful Servant
    f) John 17:1-26   Christ's Prayer

CONCLUSION "To pray is to change. Prayer is the central avenue God uses to transform us. If we are unwilling to change, we will abandon prayer as a noticeable characteristic of our lives." *(Richard Foster)*

To cease asking, To cease seeking, To cease knocking, Is to cease changing and growing!

A NEW GUIDEBOOK

II TIMOTHY 3:14-17

How To Understand The Bible

MEMORY VERSE -- *II Timothy 3:16,17*

9/31/14 - S.S. class

Traveling alone in unfamiliar territory without a map is an uncertain way to go. Being a Christian changes all that. Christ becomes the guide with the Bible as the Guidebook. Jesus taught that the Word of God is our spiritual food just like bread is our physical food. Matthew 4:4

WHY SHOULD A CHRISTIAN STUDY THE BIBLE EVERYDAY? _____
_____
_____

COMPARE THE OLD LIFE WITH THE NEW LIFE:

The Old Life:	The New Life:
1. No direction	1. New pathway
2. Wrong reading materials	2. Bible & good books
3.	3.
4.	4.

God's Word must be taken in daily portions. There is no such thing as "instant growth" by reading The Bible in one setting and ignoring it for days. God is committed to the process as well as the product.   — *John Maxwell*

God has given us the Bible so that we might discover His love and learn to enjoy His presence. As a new Christian, you will begin reading the Bible regularly.

Our purpose for living as Christians is primarily twofold;
   1. To Know God,
   2. To make Him known

In this lesson, we will learn what the Bible is, how to study the Bible, and how to know God better.

The Bible is the key to knowing God since He has revealed who He is by means of Scripture. The Bible is the world's most valuable treasure and the reading of it is a person's most profitable exercise.

I. WHAT IS THE BIBLE?

1. It is a total of **66** different books written by 40 different authors over a period of 1,500 years.

2 In our memory verse, we learn that all Scripture is **breathed** by God. Discuss what that means.

  a. Matthew 4:4 tells us that the Word comes from *the mouth of God*

  b. Matthew 5:18 says that the Scripture will last until *everything is accomplished*

  c. II Peter 1:20,21 teaches that the Scripture did not come from **prophets** but from **God, as they were carried along by the Holy Spirit**.

3. What does John 17:17 say the Word of God is? *THE WORD of God is TRUTH.*

II. WHY SHOULD WE STUDY THE BIBLE?

1. I Corinthians 2:12,13 tells us that we should study the Scripture to understand _____

2. Romans 15:4 says that the Bible was written to _____
_____so we might have_____

3. Luke 24:27 shows us that we study the Word of God to find out
_____

III. HOW WILL THE STUDY OF THE SCRIPTURE HELP ME?

1. It is through Bible study that we grow in Christ and become victorious.

  a. What are we to use when fighting the devil's schemes? Ephesians 6:17
  _____

  b. How does Scripture memorization help us according to Psalm 119:11?
  _____

  c. In John 14:23 Jesus teaches us that our desire to know God's Word is based on our _____ for Him.

2. Use the form below to discover more about the Bible and what it does in our lives.

STUDY PSALM 19:7-11 and fill in the blanks.

Verse	What The Bible Is Called	Its Characteristics	What It Will Do For Me
7a	law	perfect	renews/revives
7b	statues/testimony		
8a			
8b			
9a			
9b			
10	gold & honey	valuable	sweetens life
11	A WARNING: By my OBEDIENCE I will receive a great _____.		

3. What are the results of meditating on the Word according to Psalm 1 _____

_____

CHALLENGE: FOLLOW THE BEREAN'S EXAMPLE   Acts 17:10,11

1. They read with an open mind
2. They examined the Scriptures
3. They searched daily
   a. Joshua 1:8   c. Psalm 119:97
   b. Job 23:12   d. Jeremiah 15:16

QUESTION: WHAT TRUTH FROM GOD'S WORD HAS ESPECIALLY HELPED YOU RECENTLY? _____

_____

_____

APPLICATION: Establish a T.A.W.G. - Time Alone With God

1. Choose a time and be consistent
2. Choose a place that is quiet and secluded
3. Have a plan
   a. Begin with prayer
   b. Mark your Bible
   c. Choose a favorite verse each day and mark "FV"
   d. Pray for yourself and others using that verse.

FOR FURTHER STUDY:

1. What is said about the Word of God in John 17:17? _____

_____

2. What does the study of the Scripture offer us? Romans 15:4 _____

_____

3. How did Jesus resist the devil in Matthew 4:4, 7, 10? _____

_____

4. If one belongs to God, what does he do about God's Word? John 8:47 _____

_____   _____

5. What will God's Word do for us according to:

   a. II Timothy 3:15? _____

   b. John 15:3? _____

   c. Acts 20:32? _____

6. According to I Corinthians 8:1, what happens when we have knowledge without love? _____

_____

7. List the things from II Timothy 3:14-17 that the Word of God is profitable for:

_____

CONCLUSION: Here are some keys to follow in your reading and study of
God's Word.

1. Realize that God is sending us His love through letters of instruction,
   encouragement and consolation.
2. Read the Bible over and over again.
3. In your special time and your spare time, meditate on the Word of God.
4. Compare scripture with scripture.
5. Pray and study when you do not understand it.

A NEW FREEDOM

How To Be Forgiven

MEMORY VERSE -- I John 1:9

Although victory over sin is rightfully yours, there will be times when you miss God's perfect will. Whenever one fails or sins, Satan will immediately condemn, "Now you've really messed up. God hates you." However, in His Word, God makes provision for His children who sin and come short of His glory as we see in our memory verse. I John 1:9. Forgiveness is being reconciled on the basis of obedience.

HOW DOES THE NEW BELIEVER HANDLE GUILT? _____
_____
_____

COMPARE THE OLD LIFE WITH THE NEW LIFE:

The Old Life:
1. Living under condemnation
2. Guilty
3.
4.

The New Life:
1. Living without condemnation
2. Forgiven
3.
4.

We receive God's full forgiveness as we confess our sins to Him. To confess a sin means to uncover it and call it exactly what God calls it. This honest confession must include a willingness to forsake the sin. God promises not only to forgive us but also to cleanse us from all unrighteousness. In this lesson you will study how to experience a new freedom through forgiveness.

I. FORGIVENESS OF SIN CAN BE OURS BECAUSE OF THE NATURE OF GOD.

1. How is God described in Psalm 86:5? _____

2. In the same verse, how does He respond when we confess? _____
   _____

3. On what basis are we forgiven according to Ephesians 1:7? _____
   _____

4. According to I John 1:9

   a. Name 2 characteristics of God that are the basis of His dealings with man:
      (1) _____
      (2) _____

   b. Name two things God does for us when we confess:
      (1) _____
      (2) _____

5. If God loves the sinner, why does He hate sin? Romans 6:23 _____
   _____

6. Because of God's attitude, what should be our attitude toward those who
   have offended us? Ephesians 4:32 _____
   _____

7. Should one continue to feel guilty about sin after it has been confessed and
   forgiven? Isaiah 43:25 _____
   Why not? _____

II. FORGIVENESS OF SIN CAN BE OURS IF WE CONFESS OUR SIN.

1. According to Psalm 66:18, why should we confess our sin? _____
   _____

2. How should one confess? Leviticus 5:5 _____
   _____

3. When confessing, what do we say to God? _____
   _____

4. What are the two claims we should never make about sin?
   a. I John 1:8 _____
   b. I John 1:10 _____

5. Name one thing that is right to say about sin. I John 1:9 _____
   _____

6. According to Psalm 38:18, what should be our attitude toward sin? _____
   _____

7. What should accompany our confession of sin? Proverbs 28:13 _____
   _____

III. FORGIVENESS OF SIN IS ASSURED BY GOD'S PROVISIONS

1. According to Romans 5:8, how does God demonstrate His love for sinners?
   _____

2. What does "justified by His Blood" mean in Romans 5:9? _____
   _____

3. What does Romans 5:11 say we receive through Jesus? _____
   _____

CHALLENGE: FOLLOW DAVID'S EXAMPLE   Psalm and II Samuel

1. David's confession, Psalm 51

2. God's heart, Psalm 103

3. Consequences, despite forgiveness, II Samuel 12:13,14

4. God can still bring about good, II Samuel 12:24

QUESTION: HOW ARE WE TO WALK AFTER CONFESSION? I John 1:7
_____
_____

APPLICATION: Perhaps, through the study of this lesson, something has come to your mind which is hindering your fellowship with God - some sin that you have committed for which you have not asked forgiveness. If so, write down what God has spoken to you about.

_____

_____

Confess this to God, and claim the promise of I John 1:9 that He has forgiven your sin. Thank Him for His forgiveness.

FOR FURTHER STUDY:

1. What are some practical things we can do to show a forgiving attitude? _____

_____

_____

_____

2. What does Hebrews 10:12 say about Christ's sacrifice? _____

_____

3. To what extent are we to forgive others? Colossians 3:13_____

_____

4. List four observations from Romans 6 about sinning,

    a. verse 1 _____

    b. verse 6 _____

    c. verse 11 _____

    d. verse 12 _____

CONCLUSION: THE POSSIBILITY OF SIN DOES NOT MEAN THE PROBA-BILITY OF IT! - *John Maxwell*

Only the offender can ask for forgiveness . . .
Only the offended can give forgiveness . . .

MAN IS THE OFFENDER . . . GOD IS THE OFFENDED.
MAN IS THE FORGIVEN . . . GOD IS THE FORGIVER

A NEW CHALLENGE

How To Effectively Handle Temptation

MEMORY VERSE -- I Corinthians 10:13

From the moment that we receive Jesus Christ into our lives we are offered a new challenge - that of being an overcomer. I John 5:4 tells us that "everyone born of God overcomes the world." Now Christ who lives within enables us to be overcomers. (I John 4:4)

IS IT A SIN TO BE TEMPTED? _____

_____

_____

COMPARE THE OLD LIFE WITH THE NEW LIFE:

The Old Life:
1. Overcome by temptation
2. Serving the flesh
3.
4.

The New Life:
1. Overcoming temptation
2. Serving the Spirit
3.
4.

NOTICE THE DIFFERENCE:

"Testing is designed by God for your ***development***.
Temptation is designed by Satan for your ***destruction***."

"The proof of God's love for you is His faithfulness in temptation.
The proof of your love to God is your fleeing temptation."

— John Maxwell

Now that you are a Christian, you must realize that you are in a warfare (Ephesians 6:12). In this lesson we will study how to overcome Satan and the schemes he has devised to defeat us.

I. WE OVERCOME BY UNDERSTANDING THE NATURE OF TEMPTATION

1. According to I Corinthians 10:13, what is true about every temptation we face? _____

   _____

   a. Who helps us overcome temptation? _____

   _____

   b. Does God remove temptation? _____

   _____

   c. What does God offer to those who are being tempted? _____

   _____

   d. What is our part and what is God's part in overcoming temptation? _____

   _____

2. According to Hebrews 4:15, what is the difference between weakness and sin? _____

   _____

   a. How does Christ understand our temptation? _____

   _____

   b. How did Christ keep from sinning when tempted? Luke 4:4, 8, 12 _____

   _____

II. WE OVERCOME BY RECOGNIZING THE SOURCES OF TEMPTATION

1. According to James 1:13-14, where does a major source of temptation come from? _____

   _____

2. What are the three primary areas of temptation found in I John 2:15-16?

   a. _____

   b. _____

   c. _____

   Give an example of a specific temptation for each area mentioned: _____

   _____

3. In Romans 8:1-2, because of Christ's death and resurrection, what have we been freed from? _____

_____

4. In each of the following scriptures discuss what our new life in Christ gives us power over?

    a. Romans 6:22   b. Romans 8:9   c. I John 3:8

III. WE OVERCOME BY PRACTICING THE THINGS THAT KEEP TEMPTATION FROM LEADING INTO SIN

1. Matthew 6:9,13_____

2. Psalm 119:11 _____

3. James 4:7 _____

4. II Timothy 2:22_____

CHALLENGE: FOLLOW JOSEPH'S EXAMPLE   Genesis 39:6-18

1. What was Joseph tempted to do in Genesis 39:6-7?_____

2. What truths can we learn from Joseph's temptation from Genesis 39?

    a. vs. 6 _____

    b vs. 9 _____

    c. vs. 10 _____

    d. vs. 12 _____

    e. vs. 21 _____

QUESTION: HOW DOES GOD PROVIDE A WAY TO ESCAPE TEMPTATION?

APPLICATION: What is a specific temptation that you are frequently faced with?

_____

Write down how you think God will help you escape from this temptation. _____

_____

_____

FOR FURTHER STUDY:

1. From the following Scriptures, discover how God equips the believer to overcome the enemy:

   a. Ephesians 6:11 _____

   b. Matthew 4:10 _____

   c. Ephesians 6:17-18 _____

   d. Revelation 12:11 _____

2. In I Peter 5:8 what is the devil _____
   called and in verse 9 how are we to treat him _____

3. Ephesians 2:2 describes Satan as _____
   _____

4. In Matthew 13:19 what does Satan attempt to do with the Word of God? _____
   _____

5. John 8:44 tells us that we used to belong to _____
   and that he was a _____
   from the beginning, _____
   because he is the father of _____

6. What should be a Christians' first reaction to temptation? _____

7. List some ways you have been able to escape a particular temptation.
   _____

8. Have you grown stronger in Christ since you began resisting temptation?
   _____

CONCLUSION: When the pressure of temptation is strongly applied to our lives, it is time to let God be seen as He gives us victory.

Satan is a real but defeated foe through Jesus Christ. Because Christ overcame, we too can be overcomers. Overcoming Satan begins with right thinking. Philippians 4:8.

A NEW DIRECTION

How To Make Right Decisions

MEMORY VERSE -- *Proverbs 3:5,6*

Life is a daily process of decision making by which we can either glorify God or self. Whether we are a spiritual success or failure is determined by choice not by circumstance. Our decisions reveal what we are today and what we are going to become tomorrow.

WHAT IS THE GREATEST DECISION I AM FACED WITH TODAY? _____

_____

_____

COMPARE THE OLD LIFE WITH THE NEW LIFE:

The Old Life:	The New Life:
1. Self-centered choices	1. Christ-centered choices
2. Conformed to world	2. Transformed by Christ
3.	3.
4.	4.

Every new Christian has questions about the future. How will this new life work out? What about God's will for my life? Will God really lead me? How can I make right decisions?

God promises to lead as you rely on Him completely. He can guide you perfectly, because He knows all your needs and has infinite wisdom, power, and riches to give you the best life possible. As a new Christian, you will be faced with many decisions. In this lesson we will study how God helps us make the right choices in life.

I. WE CAN MAKE THE RIGHT DECISIONS IF WE UNDERSTAND GOD'S CHARACTER AND PROMISES TO US.

1. According to our memory verses, what three things are we told to do?

   a. _____

   b. _____

   c. _____

2. When we do our part, what does God promise He will do in Proverbs 3:6b?
   _____

3. Why should we not try to make decisions on human reasoning alone?
   Isaiah 55:8,9 _____

4. What is the warning that God gives to those who trust in human strength?
   Jeremiah 17:5 _____

5. What does God do for those who trust Him?   Isaiah 41:10
   _____

II. WE CAN MAKE RIGHT DECISIONS IF WE ARE WALKING IN OBEDIENCE TO GOD.

1. What relationship, described in John 14:10, did Jesus maintain in order to make wise decisions? _____

2. Romans 12:1,2 gives us the steps to take to experience God's will.

   a. _____

   b. _____

   c. _____

3. Discuss how our minds are renewed? _____
   _____
   _____

III. WE MUST REALIZE THAT EVERY DECISION HAS A CONSEQUENCE

1. Consequence of a wrong choice.
   Read about David in II Samuel 11.

2. Consequence of a right choice.
   Read about Joseph in Genesis 39.

IV. DISCUSS THESE SIX STEPS TO A RIGHT DECISION

1. Pray and ask for wisdom. James 1:5
2. Base decisions upon the whole counsel of God. II Timothy 3:16,17
3. Think through the consequences of your decision.
4. Consider all the options.
5. Choose the right time to make the decision.
6. Confirm you decision.
   a. Seek spiritual counsel from godly people.
      Proverbs 11:14 and Hebrews 13:17
   b. Rely on the Holy Spirit's direction.
      I Corinthians 2:12

CHALLENGE: FOLLOW MOSES'S EXAMPLE   Exodus

1. Moses began his journey with God the same as we do, fearful and lacking understanding. Exodus 2:12

2. Moses learned that God is more trustworthy than his own feelings. Exodus 15:11-13

QUESTION: HOW CAN I MAKE RIGHT DECISIONS? _____
_____
_____

APPLICATION:

1. List some aspects of your life to apply making the right decision . . .
   Job, leisure time, spending money, Christian ministry

2. Select one area and discuss how you can better acknowledge God's leadership of your life.

FOR FURTHER STUDY:

1. Discuss the significance of these three decisions:

   a. Which God will you serve?

   b. Which person will you marry?

   c. Which vocation will you follow?

2. How does the decision to make Christ Lord affect all areas of our lives.
   Romans 12:1,2 _____
   _____

3. Describe a situation which confronts you presently in which you need to seek
   God's guidance._____
   _____

CONCLUSION: Continually apply these 12 Scriptural tests to all thoughts, words
and actions.

    1. The PURITY Test – 1 Cor. 6:19
       Can I do this to the body where Christ dwells?
    2. The PARTICIPATION Test – 1 John 2:15-16
       By doing this, will I take my eyes off Jesus?
    3. The POLITE Test – Romans 14:7,21
       How will doing this affect others?
    4. The PARTNER Test – Col. 3:17
       Could I invite Christ to do this with me?
    5. The PUBLIC Test – I Thess. 5:22
       Will doing this give the appearance of wrong doing?
    6. The PRESENCE Test – 1 John 2:28
       Would I be ashamed to be found doing this upon Christ's return?
    7. The PROBLEM Test – Heb. 12:1
       Will this hinder my New Life in Christ?
    8. The PROOF Test – Romans 12:9
       Does doing this improve my capacity to hate evil and love good?
    9. The PROCLAMATION Test – Philippians 2:15
       Will doing this void my witness for Christ?
    10. The PEACE Test – Philippians 4:6-7
       After praying about it, can I do it and have peace?
    11. The PASSION Test – Mark 12:29
       Will this keep me from loving God as I should?
    12. The PRIORITY Test – Matthew 6:33
       Will this keep me from putting God first in my life?

A NEW BEHAVIOR

How To Improve Relationships

MEMORY VERSE -- John 13:35

How we relate to one another greatly determines the extent of our happiness. Everyone needs the affirmation of a healthy relationship. Becoming a Christian is the beginning of a new basis for relating to others. Just as we have received love, acceptance and forgiveness from Christ, we must freely give to others.

HOW HAS BECOMING A CHRISTIAN AFFECTED MY RELATIONSHIP WITH OTHERS?

_____

_____

_____

COMPARE THE OLD LIFE WITH THE NEW LIFE:

The Old Life:
1. Fear of rejection
2. Broken relationships
3.
4.

The New Life:
1. Feeling of affirmation
2. Building relationships
3.
4.

Each person holds the key as to whether a relationship will be hurtful or helpful. One must receive love before he can give love. Unconditional love is the only soil where a healthy relationship can grow. When a relationship turns sour, one feels like an uprooted plant. In this lesson we will study how a Christian can build and maintain healthy relationships with others.

I. DEALING WITH DIFFICULT RELATIONSHIPS

1. How does the new Christian identify and discern unprofitable relationships? II Corinthians 6:14-16 _____

_____

2. Can relationships break down between Christians? Acts 15:37-39 _____

_____

_____

2. What are some ways the new believer should handle a relationship problem?

_____

   A. Realize that one may feel bad about a bad relationship. John 13:21

   _____

   B. Uncover the problem. John 13:26

   _____

   C. Expect a response. John 13:30

   _____

   D. Allow God to be glorified. John 13:31

   _____

II. BUILDING RELATIONSHIPS ON SOLID FOUNDATIONS

1. Who is our greatest example of proper relationships? John 13:34 _____

_____

_____

2. What are some ways we should follow Christ's example in building relationships? John 13:35 _____

_____

_____

3. According to John 13:37-38, when do actions speak louder than words? ___

_____

_____

III. DISCOVERING THE BENEFITS OF GOOD RELATIONSHIPS

1. How does communication affect a relationship? John 13:33 _____

   _____

   _____

   _____

   "Tenderness without truthfulness is to be a coward.
   Truthfulness without tenderness is to be calloused.
   Tenderness with truthfulness is to be a Christian."

2. In what ways does spiritual maturity help us accept the unacceptable in relationship? John 13:36-37 _____

   _____

   _____

   Discuss These Relationship Possibilities:
   a. Some relationships will never be great
   b. Some relationships weaken over the years.
   c. Some relationships strengthen over the years.

3. According to John 13:35, how does the world know we are Christians? _____

   _____

   _____

CHALLENGE: FOLLOW THE EXAMPLE OF BARNABAS   Acts 11:22

1. He was not afraid of new relationships.
2. He realized the risk of relationships.
3. He was the aggressor in building relationships.
4. He ministered through good relationships.

QUESTION: DO I HAVE ANY RELATIONSHIPS THAT NEED SPECIAL ATTENTION?

APPLICATION:

1. Attitude is more important than action.
2. Adversity is motivator of a great relationship.
3. Greatest relationship possible because of the Blood of Christ.

FOR FURTHER STUDY:

1. Read Ephesians 2:14-18 and find the barrier that blocks relationships. _____

_____

2. What was Paul trying to get the early believers to do in Ephesians 4:2,3? _____

_____

3. In Colossians 3:15, what does the "Peace of Christ" call us to do? _____

_____

4. What attitude makes it possible for us to have good relationships with other Christians? Philippians 2:1-5 _____

_____

5. In what ways have you experienced love from fellow Christians? _____

_____

6. In what ways have you shown love to fellow believers? _____

_____

7. Discuss these four reasons why so many *flee* instead of *face* relationship problems.

   A. Rejection
   B. Hurt
   C. Pride
   D. Risk

CONCLUSION:

"Right relationships begin with character not feelings. Right relationships blossom with Grace not grit."

— *John Maxwell*

"Love as Jesus loves means experiencing God's own love in our relationships with each other. It means constantly showing that we value and care for one another as persons...not because of what is done to 'earn' acceptance. Loving each other opens up our lives to the ministry of the Holy Spirit, freeing us to grow and change and learn. Lack of love closes us off to each other...and to God."

— *Larry Richards*

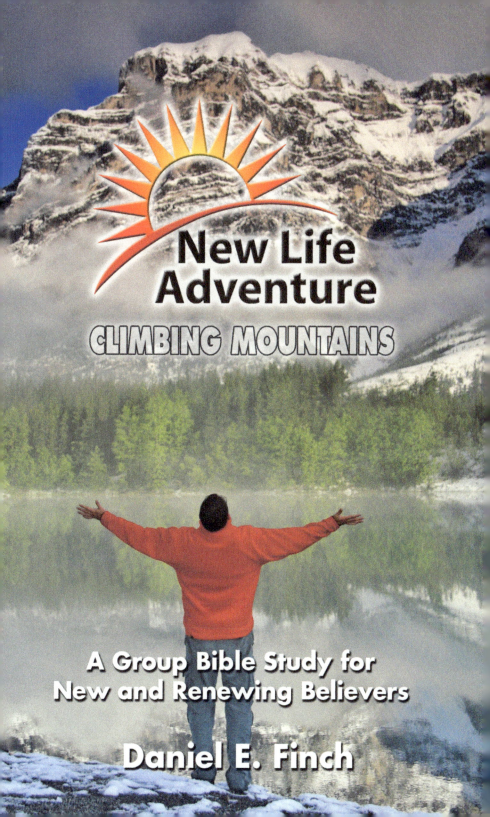

New Life Adventure

CLIMBING MOUNTAINS

A Group Bible Study for
New and Renewing Believers

Daniel E. Finch

Are you new to the Christian Faith?

Do you want to Learn more about the Bible?

Welcome to your *New Life Adventure — Climbing Mountains!* Your life has been changed by the most important decision anyone could ever make. Both how you live now and where you will live forever have been dramatically affected by this choice.

Let this Bible Study Booklet serve as your growth guide to your new life in Christ as you connect with other believers in a small group Bible Study.

Discover how your Life in Christ is different from your life outside of Christ and how you can grow in seven ways:

1. A New You 5
How To Know Who You Really Are — II Corinthians 5:17-20

2. A New Master 9
How To Be Led By God — Matthew 6:19-24,33

3. A New Community 13
How To Grow Spiritually With Others — Hebrews 10:19-25

4. A New View 17
How To Benefit From Adversity — Romans 8:28-31

5. A New Power 21
How To Be Filled With The Holy Spirit — Ephesians 5:18

6. A New Opportunity 25
How To Share Your Faith — Acts 1:8

7. A New Investment 29
How To Give Cheerfully — Romans 14:12

*"Grow in grace and
knowledge of our
Lord Jesus Christ"*
2 Peter 3:16

"BEHOLD ALL THINGS ARE BECOME NEW." II Corinthians 5:17

Congratulations

You are now part of a wonderful adventure - THE NEW LIFE! At last you have found an eternal friend, Jesus Christ. The NEW LIFE you have in Him is described in the Bible in a variety of ways. You are now a "NEW CREATION," with a "NEW MIND," a "NEW HEART." and a "NEW LIFE." The Bible also portrays the Believer as one who was dead in sin, but brought back to LIFE. You are ALIVE unto God.

The simplest and most beautiful description of what has happened to you is where Jesus compares your NEW LIFE to being "Born." Seeing a child born is exciting. It is dramatic, unique, and yet it is only the beginning. Jesus says we are "BORN again" when He comes into our lives. Your new commitment to Him has made you a NEW person. And like the baby, you must grow and mature. Babies are not born running or talking, nor do they have a college degree. They must learn to walk, talk, grow, and develop. That is the excitement of living.

The Christian life is very similar. Think of yourself as a NEW PERSON, a baby just beginning to grow. Say to yourself, "I am growing, I am learning, I am discovering. I am searching." As you do these things, you will grow, and GROW, AND GROW.

I Peter 2:2 says, "Like newborn babies, crave pure spiritual milk, so that by it you may grow up in your salvation, now that you have tasted that the LORD is good."

There are many opportunities for spiritual growth. One of the best places to learn about the Christian Life is the NEW LIFE ADVENTURE group study. Here you will discover how your NEW LIFE IN CHRIST is manifested and the ways your life will change.

Ephesians 4:22 says, "You were taught with regard to your former way of life, to put off your old self ... To be made NEW in the attitude of your minds, and to put on the NEW self, created to be like God in true righteousness and holiness.

BIBLE STUDY GUIDE

WHY STUDY THE BIBLE?
    Because God reveals Himself through His Word

THE BIBLE IS
    A ROAD MAP – to show us the way
    A LOVE LETTER – to express God's love for us
    A SEED – to help us reproduce God in others
    A SWORD – to war against the forces of evil

"The Bible is the source for our complete equipment to effectively serve the LORD."

God has some goals for each of us. He wants us to change, to grow, to mature and to affect others. The best way for all this to happen is through BIBLE STUDY.

These five methods of Scripture intake help you get a firm grasp on God's Word	
Hear	*Romans 10:17*
Read	*Revelation 1:3*
Study	*Acts 17:11*
Memorize	*Psalm 119:9-11*
Meditate	*Psalm1:2-3*

HERE ARE SOME TIPS . . .

1. Read prayerfully
2. Read with an open mind
3. Read with pen and marker. Underline or mark important words
   Write ideas/summary on Bible Study Page
4. Read to apply to all areas of life

BE ON THE LOOKOUT FOR . . .

1. Keywords
2. Repeated words
3. Strong action words
4. Advice/warnings

5. Progression of ideas
6. Commands
7. Promises I John 5:10-13

The Bookcase of The 66 Books of the Bible

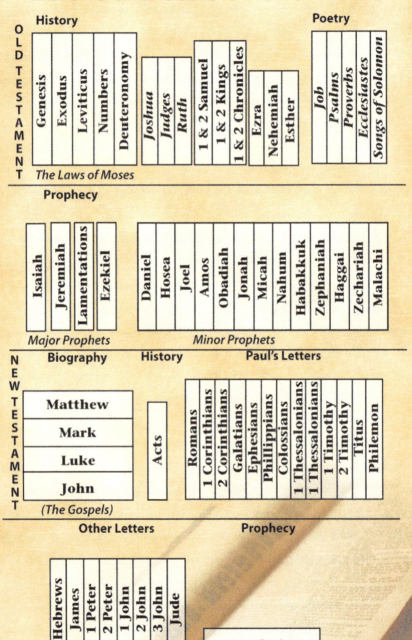

OLD TESTAMENT

History

Genesis | Exodus | Leviticus | Numbers | Deuteronomy

The Laws of Moses

Joshua | Judges | Ruth

1 & 2 Samuel | 1 & 2 Kings | 1 & 2 Chronicles

Ezra | Nehemiah | Esther

Poetry

Job | Psalms | Proverbs | Ecclesiastes | Songs of Solomon

Prophecy

Isaiah | Jeremiah | Lamentations | Ezekiel

Major Prophets

Daniel | Hosea | Joel | Amos | Obadiah | Jonah | Micah | Nahum | Habakkuk | Zephaniah | Haggai | Zechariah | Malachi

Minor Prophets

NEW TESTAMENT

Biography

Matthew | Mark | Luke | John

(The Gospels)

History

Acts

Paul's Letters

Romans | 1 Corinthians | 2 Corinthians | Galatians | Ephesians | Phillippians | Colossians | 1 Thessalonians | 1 Thessalonians | 1 Timothy | 2 Timothy | Titus | Philemon

Other Letters

Hebrews | James | 1 Peter | 2 Peter | 1 John | 2 John | 3 John | Jude

Prophecy

Revelation

A NEW YOU

How To Know Who You Really Are

MEMORY VERSE -- *II Corinthians 5:17*

You are special. You did not begin your Christian life by reformation but by transformation. It is not simply turning over a new leaf but receiving an entirely new life. Christ imparts His life to us. The NEW YOU will then begin to think like Jesus and consequently act like Jesus. That is why the new believer is called a Christian.

WHAT CHANGES IN YOUR PERSONALITY ARE EVIDENT SINCE YOU BECAME A CHRISTIAN? _____

_____

_____

_____

COMPARE THE OLD LIFE WITH THE NEW LIFE:

The Old Life:

1. Feel Rejected by God
2. Living outside of Christ
3.
4.

The New Life:

1. Feel Accepted by God
2. Living inside Christ
3.
4.

Becoming a Christian does not reduce one into nonpersonhood, but it enhances the individual by creating a brand new person through whom the love of Jesus is revealed.

To be called a child of God (I John 3:1) indicates both a privilege and responsibility as we are changed into a new person. In this lesson we will study about "who we really are in Christ."

I. IN CHRIST ONE HAS A NEW POSITION Vs. 17

"We are in Christ and Christ is in us."

1. What does this verse say about a brand new beginning to life?_____
   _____
   _____

2. What does II Corinthians 5:21 tell us we become as we live and grow in
   Christ?_____
   _____
   _____

3. Name several things that happen as a result of our being in Christ in
   Ephesians 1:7,8. _____
   _____
   _____

4. What does Colossians 2:9,10 say we are given when we are in Christ? _____
   _____
   _____

II. IN CHRIST ONE HAS NEW POSSESSIONS Vs. 17

1. List several aspects of the old life that must be discarded. _____
   _____
   _____

2. List several things that are added as the result of the new life. _____
   _____
   _____

3. According to II Peter 1:2-4 what is the extent of what is added to the believer
   in Christ?_____
   _____
   _____

III. IN CHRIST ONE HAS NEW POTENTIAL Vs. 18

1. What is the basis of our new relationship with Christ?_____

   _____

   _____

2. What is the new ministry that we are now able to be involved in?_____

   _____

   _____

IV. IN CHRIST ONE HAS A NEW PURPOSE Vs. 20

1. You know what to do. We are to be Christ's_____

   _____

2. You know how to do it. We are to share the message of _____

   _____

"In Christ we move from consumer to contributor."

CHALLENGE: FOLLOW GIDEON'S EXAMPLE   Judges 7:7-15

1. God made Gideon more than he was otherwise. vs. 12
2. God used Gideon even with his limitations. vs. 14
3. Gideon became the man God expected him to be. vs.15

"When we are given the name "Christian",
God expects us to grow up into all that name stands for."

QUESTION: HOW HAS MY NEW FAITH IN CHRIST BROUGHT ABOUT A
RADICAL TRANSFORMATION? _____

_____

APPLICATION:

1. Ask a Christian friend to help you pray about an attitude or habit that you need
   to be free from.

2. Find a non-Christian friend that you can begin to share the message of
   reconciliation with.

3. Daily affirm your new life in Christ by continually thinking "I am now a new
   person living in Christ."

FOR FURTHER STUDY:

1. According to Romans 12:2, what does the beginning of the transformation to a new life begin with? _____

_____
_____

2. Do we need to try to get God to like us?   Ephesians 1:6

_____
_____

3. Even though we know the world's judgments of us are unreliable,   I John 4:5 why is our self-concept largely determined by the world? _____

_____
_____

4. What physical problems did Paul have to overcome in II Corinthians 10:10?

_____
_____

5. What must be continually added to our faith?   II Peter 1:5-7

_____
_____

CONCLUSION: Self-realization only comes as we learn more of God not when we learn more of self. Discovery of who we are in Christ mandates a willingness to change. The New Life is revealed as we are daily transformed into His image.

"To discover my uniqueness and become what God intended me to be, I must give myself away recklessly, lavishly. The greatest gift you have to give is yourself."

– Bruce Larson

A NEW MASTER

How To Be Led By God

MEMORY VERSE -- Matthew 6:33

When we become a Christian, we change masters and begin to live under new ownership. Because we have surrendered the control of our lives to Christ, He becomes the new ruler. Even though He becomes our Savior at conversion, He also wants to become our Sovereign Lord and Master. We can only enjoy our New Life in Christ as we daily seek His will and walk in obedience to His leading.

WHY DOES A PERSON TRY TO BE HIS OWN MASTER? _____

_____

_____

_____

COMPARE THE OLD LIFE WITH THE NEW LIFE:

The Old Life:
1. Satan as ruler
2. Bondage
3.
4.

The New Life:
1. Christ as Lord
2. Liberty
3.
4.

When Christ is invited into our lives, He comes as a guest. However, it is possible to be forgiven and yet have a divided heart. It is only by making Christ LORD OF ALL that we will be led by our New Master. The key to the leadership of God is the Lordship of Christ. In this lesson we will study what it means to have a New Master and follow His leading.

*"UNTIL A COMMITMENT IS MADE TO ONE MASTER,
THE EYE WILL ALWAYS BE ROVING TO FIND GREENER PASTURE."*

I. THE DISASTER OF TRYING TO SERVE TWO MASTERS

*"We become miserable when a noble cause before us
reveals a divided heart within us."*

1. What conflicting attitudes arise when we try to serve two masters? Matthew 6:24

_____

_____

2. What are some results of a divided heart?

a. _____   James 1:8

b. _____   Romans 7:15

c. _____   Romans 7:18

d. _____   Romans 7:19

e. _____   Romans 7:23

3. Why do we try to serve two masters? Find the answer in Matthew 6:22,23

_____

_____

_____

_____

"What we SEE is what we SEEK"

II. THE DECISION TO MAKE CHRIST LORD OF ALL

Life's Living Option:

Every man has a choice to make.
Every man has the ability to make that choice.
Every man lives the life he chooses.
Every man receives the consequence of that choice.

1. What did Joshua challenge the people to do who were trying
to serve two Masters?   Joshua 24:14,15

_____

2. How did Elijah deal with those who were undecided about
which God to serve?   I Kings 18:21-37

_____

III. THE DESIRE TO KEEP CHRIST FIRST IN EVERYTHING

1. Our part in Matthew 6:33 is to _____

   _____

   God's part in Matthew 6:33 is to _____

2. What are the benefits of seeking first the kingdom of God?   Matthew 6:33

   _____

3. How does our choice to make Christ Lord change our priorities? Matthew 6:33

   _____

4. In what ways does "new ownership" lead us to "new relationship?"   Rev. 3:20

   _____

5. How did Jesus deal with the temptation to serve two Masters? Matthew 4:8-10

   _____

CHALLENGE: FOLLOW PAUL'S EXAMPLE   Philippians 3:7-14

1. Loyalty to wrong master is useless. Vs.7
2. Knowing Christ is of greatest importance. Vs. 10
3. Persistence does not insure perfection. Vs. 12
4. Energies are narrowed to one direction. Vs. 13
5. Dealing with the past through forgetfulness Vs. 13
6. Stretching toward the goal. Vs. 13,14

QUESTION: IS JESUS LORD OF ALL YOUR LIFE? _____

_____
_____
_____

APPLICATION: APPLY THE QUESTION ABOVE TO THE FOLLOWING AREAS OF YOUR LIFE:

a. vocation plans   e. spiritual gifts
b. material possessions   f. sex life
c. affections & relationships   g. habits
d. responsibility   h. other areas

FOR FURTHER STUDY:

1. A good way to make Christ Lord of your life is to continually ask the question, "What would Jesus do in this situation?"

Situation	Jesus would:
a.	a.
b.	b.
c.	c.

2. According to I Samuel 7:3, what is the condition of God's deliverance from the control of the enemy? _____

_____

_____

3. In I Peter 3:15, how does one make Christ Lord? _____

_____

_____

4. Discuss what is wrong with today's concept that "Man has finally become mature enough to be his own master." _____

_____

_____

5. Read Robert Munger's "My Heart - Christ's Home." _____

_____

_____

CONCLUSION: Every person eventually comes to the crossroads of choosing which master will claim his undivided loyalty. Blessed is the one that abdicates the throne and surrenders totally to the lordship of Christ. This simply means we are not our own, we belong to Him. Christ is fully in control. He calls the plays and we run with the ball. We depend totally on His resources for our spiritual victory.

A NEW COMMUNITY

How To Grow Spiritually With Others

MEMORY VERSE -- Hebrews 10:24,25

Now that you have become a Christian, it is only natural for you to want to be with fellow believers. The best way to discover new friends who also love Jesus and to become a part of the family of God is to attend church.

WHAT DOES CHURCH MEAN TO YOU? _____

_____

_____

_____

COMPARE THE OLD LIFE WITH THE NEW LIFE:

The Old Life:	The New Life:
1. Worldly interests	1. Christian interests
2. Attend church occasionally	2. Attend church regularly
3.	3.
4.	4.

How exciting it is to find a whole new family. Every true Christian is your brother or sister. This new family is the church which the Bible calls the Body of Christ. Be sure to show your spiritual family plenty of love.

Usually the first thing Paul did when visiting a town was to find and attend church, (Acts 18:19). Today we will study why a good church is important for fellowship, inspiration, and spiritual instruction.

I. CHURCH ATTENDANCE IS IMPORTANT BECAUSE GOD COMMANDS IT

1. What 2 things does Hebrews 10:24,25 tell us will be the result of the believers assembling together?

   a. _____

   b. _____

2. What does Hebrews 10:25 challenge us to not do?_____
   _____

3. What word in Hebrews 10:25 suggests regular church attendance?_____
   _____

4. Do you think a Christian is ever tempted to not go to church? _____
   _____
   _____

II. CHURCH ATTENDANCE IS MODELED BY THE NEW TESTAMENT CHURCH

1. In Acts 2:41-47, what four things was the church devoted to?

   a. Devoted to _____

   b. Devoted to _____

   c. Devoted to _____

   d. Devoted to _____

2. What one concept do the following scriptures have in common?

   a. Acts 1:6   f. Acts 15:30
   b. Acts 2:1   g. Acts 20:7,8
   c. Acts 10:27   h. I Corinthians 5:4
   d. Acts 12:12   i. Ephesians 2:6
   e. Acts 14:27   j. Acts 4:31

III. CHURCH ATTENDANCE BRINGS THE BODY OF CHRIST TOGETHER

1. Who is the Head of the church?   Ephesians 5:23
   _____

2. How important is the Church to Jesus Christ?   Ephesians 5:25
   _____

3. What phrase in I Corinthians 12:27 teaches us that we should work in harmony together as Christians? _____

_____

4. Are all members the same?   Romans 12:4

_____

5. What is the relationship of one member to another?   Romans 12:5

_____

6. How does one member's "hurts" affect the rest of the body? I Corinthians 12:14-26

_____

7. What attitude should members have toward each other?   Romans 12:10

_____

8. How should I treat a fellow member of the church?   Galatians 6:2

_____

IV. CHURCH ATTENDANCE OFFERS PARTICIPATION IN THE ORDINANCES

1. Baptism   Romans 6:3
2. Communion   I Corinthians 11:24-28

CHALLENGE: Some churches are powerful and loving, and some are not. Which of the following two churches is like the one you would wish to belong to?

1. The church at Philadelphia.   Revelation 3:7-13
2. The church at Laodicea.   Revelation 3:14-22

QUESTION: HOW WILL THE WORLD KNOW THAT   John 13:35
I BELONG TO THE TRUE CHURCH?

_____
_____
_____

APPLICATION:

1. Worship regularly in a church that is true to the Scriptures.
2. Contact the pastor about baptism.
3. Commit yourself to the local body of believers by becoming a member.

FOR FURTHER STUDY:

1. What is the attitude of the Church to the authority of Christ?   Ephesians 5:24

_____

2. According to Mark 16:15 what is the primary goal of the church?_____

_____

3. What should a person do with a part of his income each week? I Corinthians 16:2

_____

4. What attitude should we have when giving to the church?   II Corinthians 9:7

_____

5. What does God say in Isaiah 56:7 that His house should be called?_____

_____

6. What does I Timothy 3:15 say the church is?_____

_____

7. What does Matthew 28:19,20 tell us that the mission of the church should be?

_____

CONCLUSION:

"The church is not a physical building, but a group of believers; not a denomination, sect or association, but a spiritual body. The church is not an organization, but a communion, a fellowship of one body, and it includes all believers."

– John MacArthur

Christ and the early Christians were known for their love for one another. So we as Christians today, individually and collectively as a church, should be known for our love. The early church was also known for its intensive spirit of outreach. This strong conviction and commitment will bond us together in effectively manifesting the love of Jesus to our unbelieving world.

A NEW VIEW

How To Benefit From Adversity

MEMORY VERSE -- *Romans 8:28*

Often bad things happen to good people. Since the fall of Adam, pain and suffering have been in the world. Becoming a Christian does not exempt one from adversity, yet the new believer draws upon a new source of strength. God has promised to uphold His children with His hand.

HOW HAS GOD USED SUFFERING IN YOUR LIFE TO HELP YOU?

_____

_____

_____

COMPARE THE OLD LIFE WITH THE NEW LIFE:

The Old Life:	The New Life:
1. Hopelessness in trouble	1. Confidence in God
2. Depression	2. Assurance
3.	3.
4.	4.

Sometimes when we suffer loss, we are tempted to ask, "Why" and grow bitter. The Bible gives us some definite ways we can profit from suffering, and become spiritually enriched. In this lesson we will study how we can benefit spiritually when we experience suffering.

I. THE CAUSE OF SUFFERING

God did not plan suffering and death for His world. To discover the source of all sorrow read Genesis 3 and discuss the following questions.

1. What does Genesis 2:15-17 say that God originally planned for man?

    _____

2. According to Genesis 3:4-5, who tempted Eve to eat the forbidden fruit?

    _____

3. Because Adam & Eve sinned, what happened to them in Genesis 3:16-24?

    _____

4. Who then is to blame for all the suffering in the world? _____

    _____

II. THE CHRISTIAN IS NOT EXEMPT FROM SUFFERING

1. What often accompanies a persons faith in Christ?   Philippians 1:29 (NASB)

    _____

2. What is promised to those who live godly lives?   II Timothy 3:12

    _____

3. What should be our attitude toward suffering?   James 1:2

    _____

III. THE PURPOSE OF SUFFERING

1. How is suffering beneficial for spiritual progress?   Psalms 119:67

    _____

2. How does affliction help us to comfort others?   II Corinthians 1:3-7

    _____

3. According to Philippians 1:12, what was the result of Paul's adversity?

    _____

4. Discuss the fourfold aspect of God's purpose:

    a. God's purpose is inclusive ... "all things"
    b. God's purpose is active ... "work"
    c. God's purpose is harmonious ... "together"
    d. God's purpose is beautiful ... "for good"

IV. THE COMPARISON BETWEEN PRESENT SUFFERINGS AND COMING GLORY

"Bearing the cross proceeds wearing the crown"

1. According to II Corinthians 4:17 what is the relationship of present suffering to eternal glory? _____

_____

2. In II Corinthians 5:1, what are we promised when life's sufferings are over?

_____

_____

CHALLENGE: FOLLOW JOB'S EXAMPLE   Job

Job is the all-time example for those who suffer.

1. He suffered ridicule from his wife
2. He suffered scorning from his friends
3. He suffered the loss of his property
4. He suffered the death of his children
5. He suffered the loss of his influence
6. He suffered the loss of his health

In spite of all Job's suffering, what did he say about his commitment to serve God in Job 13:15?_____

_____

_____

QUESTION: HOW CAN I BE AN OVERCOMER DURING ADVERSITY

_____

_____

_____

_____

APPLICATION:

1. Ask a fellow-believer how he has overcome suffering in his life.
2. Find a Bible character who suffered and discover how he was victorious.

FOR FURTHER STUDY:

1. Read Psalms 119:67 & 119:71. How did this man benefit from suffering?

_____

_____

2. From Hebrews 12:5-8 we discover that God's correction is a reminder of His

_____

_____

3. What kind of suffering is Jesus speaking about in Luke 6:22-23?

_____

_____

4. What is commendable before God according to I Peter 2:19-20?

_____

_____

5. Summarize what I Peter 2:21-23 teaches about the example of Christ.

_____

_____

6. Read Romans 12:19. Why should we not seek revenge when we suffer?

_____

_____

7. What did the apostles do when they were called upon to   Acts 5:40-41
   suffer for Jesus?

_____

_____

CONCLUSION: Yes, there is suffering now, but we must understand that God will eventually bring the world back to His original will – a new heaven and earth without suffering. In the meantime, we must recognize God as loving and wise. Let us trust God in our sufferings. Let us realize that He has a purpose – even though we may not see it. Let us sing with the songwriter, "For I know what'er befalls me, Jesus doeth all things well."

A NEW POWER

How To Be Filled With The Holy Spirit

MEMORY VERSE -- Ephesians 5:18

Coming to know Christ is the greatest event one can ever experience. The Holy Spirit brings a person to Christ and continues to dwell with that person. However, after conversion, the believer often experiences defeat and fruitlessness. Even though he has the Holy Spirit, the Holy Spirit does not have all of the believer. It is possible for the believer to be filled with the Holy Spirit and walk in spiritual power.

IN WHAT WAY DO I EXPERIENCE SPIRITUAL DEFEAT? _____
_____
_____

COMPARE THE LIFE BEFORE BEING FILLED WITH THE SPIRIT AND AFTER BEING FILLED WITH THE SPIRIT:

BEFORE:
1. Little fruit
2. Coward
3.
4.

AFTER:
1. Much fruit
2. Courageous
3.
4.

The New Testament refers to the Holy Spirit nearly 300 times. "Power" is the one word which is continually associated with the Holy Spirit. The process of being filled and controlled by God's Spirit could be explained like this:

What I give Him – He takes
　　What He takes – He cleanses
　　　　What He cleanses – He fills with His Spirit
　　　　　　What He fills – He anoints with His power
　　　　　　　　What He anoints with His power – He uses effectively!

Today we will study how the Holy Spirit works in our lives.

I. BEFORE CONVERSION

1. John 16:8 teaches us that the Holy Spirit _____

_____

2. According to John 16:13-15, the Holy Spirit _____

_____

II. WHEN ONE BECOMES A CHRISTIAN

1. What does John 6:63 say the Holy Spirit does? _____

_____

2. How does the Holy Spirit give assurance of salvation?   Romans 8:16

_____

III. AFTER ONE IS BORN AGAIN

1. Ephesians 4:30 tells us not to _____

_____

2. Ephesians 5:18 commands us to _____

_____

IV. HOW IS THE FULLNESS OF THE SPIRIT RECEIVED?

1. Ask God to give you the Holy Spirit in His fullness.   Luke 11:13

2. Yield your whole life to God.   Romans 12:1,2

3. Admit your need for inner cleansing and purity.   Acts 15:8,9

4. Receive the sanctifying spirit by an act of faith.   I Thessalonians 5:23,24

V. AFTER ONE IS FILLED WITH THE HOLY SPIRIT

1. Jesus taught His disciples that the Holy Spirit would come to   John 14:17
live with them and be _____

2. In John 14:26 Jesus assured His disciples that He would send the Holy Spirit to
them to _____

3. Acts 1:8 shows us that when we receive the fullness of the Holy Spirit we will
be endued with _____ and we will be _____.

4. Galatians 5:22-25 tells us that the Holy Spirit will be manifested in nine ways:

1.   6.
2.   7.
3.   8.
4.   9.
5.

5. I John 4:4 teaches us that the believer is victorious because _____
_____

CHALLENGE: FOLLOW CORNELIUS' EXAMPLE   Acts 11:15-17

1. Cornelius was a devout and God fearing man.   Acts 10:1

2. Cornelius was obedient.   Acts 10:30-33

3. Cornelius received the Holy Spirit.   Acts 11:15

QUESTION: HAVE I BEEN FILLED WITH THE HOLY SPIRIT? _____
_____
_____
_____

APPLICATION: PRAY TO BE FILLED WITH THE HOLY SPIRIT:

Dear God, I need You. I want to be filled with the Holy Spirit. I admit that I have been in control of my life. I thank You for forgiving my sins. I ask You to cleanse me of this sinful, carnal nature. Right now I surrender totally to the lordship of Christ. All that I am, have, or hope to be, I surrender. I put myself completely in Your hands. I do this now as an act of faith. Please make me clean, and fill me with the Holy Spirit. Thank You for cleansing me, for filling me, and for taking control of my life. In Jesus' name I pray this. AMEN

FOR FURTHER STUDY:

1. Who did Jesus say would give us an overflowing experience? John 7:38,39

_____

_____

2. Who is our teacher of truth? John 14:26

_____

_____

3. When does the Holy Spirit begin to work in a person's life? John 3:5

_____

_____

4. Why were the Corinthians not spirit-filled? I Corinthians 3:3

_____

_____

5. What should we do with impure attitudes? II Corinthians 7:1

_____

_____

6. How complete does God wish our cleansing to be? I Thessalonians 5:23

_____

_____

7. How is my relationship with the Holy Spirit maintained? Romans 8:4

_____

_____

CONCLUSION: As we have seen in this lesson, God has provided a solution to our emptiness and fruitlessness. It is the fullness of the Holy Spirit. This full surrender to the lordship of Christ and dynamic filling of the Holy Spirit gives power for witnessing and results in fruitful, effective Christian service.

A NEW OPPORTUNITY

How To Share Your Faith

MEMORY VERSE -- Acts 1:8

One of the first reactions a person has when he receives Christ is the desire to tell others about his new found Joy. Even though the urge to witness is quite natural, new believers are often fearful to share with others.

HOW DOES A NEW BELIEVER OVERCOME FEAR WHEN SHARING HIS PERSONAL TESTIMONY WITH OTHERS? _____

_____

_____

_____

COMPARE THE OLD LIFE WITH THE NEW LIFE:

The Old Life:	The New Life:
1. Embarrassed to talk about Christ	1. Excited to talk about Christ.
2. No concern for others salvation.	2. Great concern for others salvation.
3.	3.
4.	4.

Sharing the good news about salvation is not left to choice. It is the result of a caring attitude. It is the response to Christ's command in Acts 1:8, "you shall be my witnesses." In this lesson, we will study what the Bible says about witnessing. Discover how to be a successful witness and soul-winner so you can experience the joy of leading others to Christ.

I. WHY SHOULD THE BELIEVER SHARE HIS FAITH WITH OTHERS?

1. What does Christ tell us to do in Mark 16:15? *Go into all the world & Preach the good news to all creation.*

2. According to Romans 10:13,14 before a person can call upon the Lord to be saved, what is necessary? *Believe, hear the word, Someone preach(or witness to them)*

3. Does failing to witness have any consequence for the believer according to Ezekiel 3:18-19 *God will hold you accountable for his blood.*

4. What value does Matthew 16:26 place on one soul? *what can man exchange for his soul.*

5. From what does heaven derive its greatest reason for celebration according to Luke 15:10? *angels rejoice in heaven over one soul.*

II. HOW SHOULD THE BELIEVER SHARE HIS FAITH WITH OTHERS?

1. According to Matthew 5:16, what is the basis of an effective witness for Christ? *Let your light so shine before men, that they may see you Good works and praise your father in*

2. According to Acts 1:4, how do I get the power to witness for Christ? *Heaven-wait for the gift of the Holy Spirit!*

3. An effective witness for Christ should contain at least three things:

A. THE PERSON
   Why must our witness center on Christ?   John 14:6

B. THE PERSONAL TESTIMONY
   1. A Testimony should not. . .
      a. Contain meaningless statements, facts, etc.
      b. Contain too much personal trivia.
      c. Give a "holier than thou" impression.
      d. Use technical or religious terms that are not properly defined.
      e. Be too lengthy.

   2. A Testimony should . . .
      a. Identify with the listener by discussing mutual interests.
      b. Contain honest statements.
      c. Give clear account of how you were saved.
      d. Be a personal expression of what Christ has done for you.

e. Keep Christ and the gospel central.

f. Be an illustration of Christ's faithfulness.

g. Base assurance of salvation on scripture.

h. Refrain from negative comments about persons, other churches or denominations.

C. THE PLAN

What is the reason (or learning a definite plan as taught in I Peter 3:15?

III. WHEN SHOULD THE BELIEVER SHARE HIS FAITH WITH OTHERS

1. In John 4:5-7, where was Christ when He talked with the Samaritan woman?

   By the well — offering living water

2. In Acts 11:11-14, who spoke to Peter about the men who were seeking him?

   The LORD !

3. Where did Paul meet people in order to present Christ to them? Acts 17:17; 20:20

   ATHENS(synogogue and Market place)

4. How long did Andrew wait until he shared Christ with his brother?   John 1:41

   THE SAME DAY !

5. What were the Christians doing in Acts 5:42? _Day after day, In the temple courts, house to house, they never stopped teaching and proclaiming the good News, that Jesus is the CHRIST CHILD._

CHALLENGE: FOLLOW PHILIP'S EXAMPLE   Acts 8:26-40

1. Responsive to the Holy Spirit. Vs. 26
2. Obedient to the Lord's command. Vs. 27
3. Sensitive to the Ethiopian's need. Vs. 30
4. Skilled in the Word. Vs. 35
5. Sought for a decision. Vs. 37

QUESTION: WHAT IS OUR SOURCE OF POWER AS REVEALED IN OUR MEMORY VERSE, ACTS 1:8? _____

_____

_____

APPLICATION:

1. Mark your Bible with a soul winning plan which contains at least these key verses:

   a. Knowing where you are going. John 3:3
   b. Repent. Acts 3:19
   c. Believe. John 3:16
   d. Confess. I John 1:9
   e. Receive. John 1:12
   f. Open the door. Rev. 3:20

2. List the names of three people you know need Christ, and for whom you will pray, and to whom you will witness when there is opportunity.

   _____
   _____
   _____

3. On a separate sheet of paper write out your personal testimony.

FOR FURTHER STUDY:

1. What direction to "witness" does Christ give in Luke 8:39? _____
   _____

2. Based on John 3:32, what is the believer to tell about? _____
   _____

3. What did Jesus say was God's supreme work?   John 6:29
   _____

4. What is the work Christ tells us to do in John 15:16? _____
   _____

5. What did the Samaritan woman do in John 4:28,29? _____
   _____

6. What did Jesus say He would do if we would follow Him according to Matthew 4:19? _____
   _____

7. Who shared the good news with you? _____
   _____

CONCLUSION: Everyone is not expected to be a great "soul-winner" but all are expected to be great "witnesses."

"Successful witnessing is sharing Christ in the power of the Holy Spirit and leaving the results to God."

– Bill Bright

A NEW INVESTMENT

How To Be A Cheerful Giver

> **MEMORY VERSE -- Romans 14:12**
>
>
>

Daniel Webster once wrote, "The greatest thought that ever entered my mind is the fact of my responsibility to God." One day we will face God to give an account of how we used our money, time and abilities for Him.

What are some things that keep us from giving to God? _____

_____

_____

_____

Compare the Old Life with the New Life:

The Old Life: The New Life:
1. Stingy   1. Generous
2. Don't want to give   2. Want to give
3.   3.
4.   4.

Why did Jesus say "It is more blessed to give than to receive?   Acts 20:35

_____

_____

Someone has said you can give without loving, but you cannot love without giving. We discover the same truth in spiritual things. As we love God, we will give to Him as we learn how to be good stewards of what He has given us. In this lesson, we will study what the Bible says about stewardship and how we can be good stewards.

To be a good steward we must remember the following points:

I. EVERYTHING BELONGS TO GOD

1. According to Psalm 24:1, who owns the world? _____

_____

2. To whom do we belong?   I Corinthians 6:19-20

_____

II. GOD HAS MADE US THE TRUSTEES OF HIS POSSESSIONS

1. Parable of the Tenants: Matthew 21:33-34.
   What did the landowner expect?_____

_____

2. Parable of the Talents: Matthew 25:14-30.
   What did the Master expect? _____

_____

III. OUR PRIORITIES ARE DETERMINED BY CHOICES

1. What does Matthew 6:33 have to do with giving?_____

_____

2. What does Romans 12:1 tell us we should give to God?_____

_____

IV. THERE WILL BE AN ACCOUNTING OF HOW WE MANAGED OUR LIVES AND RESOURCES

1. How well did we manage our time?   Ephesians 5:15-16

_____

2. How faithful did we work?   Ephesians 6:7-8

_____

3. What did we talk about?   Matthew 12:36

_____

4. Did we give God what He asked for?   Malachi 3:10

_____

5. How did we spend what was ours?   Luke 16:1-3

_____

6. Were we a faithful witness?   I Thessalonians 2:4

_____

WHAT ARE SOME WAYS WE SHOULD STEWARD WELL OUR RESOURCES?

_____
_____
_____

CHALLENGE: FOLLOW THE WIDOW'S EXAMPLE   Mark 12:41-44

1. In this passage who was watching as the people gave their offerings?

_____

2. How did the rich give?_____

3. How did the widow give? _____

_____

4. According to Jesus who gave the most?_____

_____

QUESTION: Are you giving all God expects you to give?

FOR FURTHER STUDY:

1. After mediating on John 3:16, does God ask more of us than He was willing to give? _____

2. We will not only be accountable for our money and our lives, but what else according to Matthew 12:36? _____

3. What are some different ways we can invest as a successful steward for God?
   _____

4. In what ways are you investing now as a good steward? _____
   _____

5. In Luke 10:30-37, we find the story of the Good Samaritan. In what ways was he a good steward?_____

We ought to give:
    1. Willingly: Acts 4:34-35
    2. Cheerfully: II Corinthians 9:7
    3. Faithfully: II Chronicles 31:11-12

Stewards are not rewarded for their production, as seen in the parable of the talents. The steward who increased five talents was rewarded the same as the steward who increased two talents. The stewards were rewarded for their faithfulness to the task.
— I Corinthians 4:2

"He is no fool who gives what he cannot keep to gain what he cannot lose."
— Jim Elliot

HISTORY OF TEAM-UP EVANGELISM

In 1980 John C. Maxwell, noted pastor and church growth leader, launched a pilot evangelism program called G.R.A.D.E. in select churches across America after he had successfully implemented it in the church where he was pastoring. In a few years this simple outreach tool was being used by hundreds of churches in over seventy denominations. G.R.A.D.E. was an acronym that stood for:

Growth Resulting After Discipleship & Evangelism

As a result, thousands of people were reached for Christ and churches began to grow. The plan for G.R.A.D.E. was simple. Train believers to be involved in the ministries of prayer, encouragement, soul-winning, and discipleship. In fact, the same principles may be ready to germinate in your church!

1. Do you have people who regularly pray for the unsaved?
2. Do you know someone who is continually reaching out with compassion to unchurched people?
3. Is there a person in your church who regularly leads others to Jesus?
4. Are there those who take a special interest in helping new believers become established in their faith?

If your answer is yes, then the basic principles of the Great Commission are already at work in your church. You may simply need to organize your people into teams, equip believers to improve skills, unify and broaden each area of ministry. You may want to look at the following resources, which could help you in that process. We have upgraded G.R.A.D.E. and it is now called……

TEAM – UP
EVANGELISM

TEAM –UP EVANGELISM

MOBILIZING THE WHOLE CHURCH

To Keep the Dream Alive

By Doing Evangelism in T E A M S....

T*ogether*

E*vangelizing*

A*nd*

M*ultiplying*

S*uccessfully*

REACHING OUT

INVITING IN

RAISING UP

No Believer Left Behind

OVERVIEW OF TEAM-UP EVANGELISM

UP G.R.A.D.E. YOUR CHURCH'S EVANGELISM FOCUS

The purpose of this Dream-UP Leader's Guide is to provide leaders with an understanding of TEAM-UP and how to recruit and launch TEAMS into an effective fulfillment of the Great Commission.

How to implement an evangelism and discipleship ministry in your church

Strategic Evangelism with four Biblical Teams

TEAM-UP is a practical system designed to assist local churches reach their greatest evangelism and follow-through potential, by mobilizing the whole church to do evangelism in four teams...

1. THE *A* TEAM : *Advance Prayer Warriors.*

People Who Pray Together for Results.

Example: ABRAHAM, WHO PRAYED FOR OTHERS.

2. THE *B* TEAM : *Bridge-Builders Brigade.*

People who Build Bridges of Compassion and Community Outreach.

Example: BARNABAS, WHO REACHED OUT TO OTHERS.

3. THE *C* TEAM: *Conversion Coaches.* People Who Help Unbelievers Come to Faith in Christ.

Example: ANDREW, WHO LED OTHERS TO CHRIST.

4. THE *D* TEAM: *Discipleship Trainers.* People who Guide New Believers in Spiritual Formation.

Example: TIMOTHY, WHO MENTORED OTHERS.

Mobilizing the Whole Church to Take the Whole Gospel to the Whole World

The *Dream* of every Pastor and the *Vision* of Every Church should be:

187

Reaching Out Inviting In Raising UP

To REACH OUT to spiritually unresolved people

To INVITE them IN to the spiritual journey, and

To RAISE UP wholehearted followers of Jesus Christ

Strategic Mobilization with Four Biblical Teams

A- TEAM: **A**DVANCE PRAYER WARRIORS

Praying Together for Results: *Modeled by*

Abraham, Who Prayed

- **Make a list of non-believers**
- **Form multiple prayer groups**
- **Intentionally pray for the salvation of non-Christians**

B- TEAM: **B**RIDGE-BUILDERS

Building Bridges of Friendship: *Modeled by*

Barnabas, who Reached Out

- **Seek involvement in the life of the community**
- **Make contact with unreached people by personal visit or other means**
- **Become a caregiving friend whenever and wherever needed**

C-TEAM: **C**ONVERSION COACHES

Helping People Come to Faith in Christ.

Modeled by Andrew, Who Was a Spiritual Guide

- Learn a plan of salvation and how to share your faith
- Engage receptive people in a discussion of spiritual things
- Know how and when to lead a person to accept Christ as Savior and Lord

D-TEAM: **D**ISCIPLESHIP TRAINERS

Guiding People in Spiritual Formation:

Modeled by TIMOTHY, Who Mentored

New Believers

- Meet and disciple new believers one-to-one
- Be available to new believers at all times
- Encourage new believers to attend a new Christians class or group

Let TEAM-UP IGNITE
A NEW FIRE OF EVANGELISM
IN YOUR CHURCH

FROM DREAMS TO TEAMS

God's Dreams for His Church:

"As You sent Me into the world, I also have sent them into the world.(v.18) That they all may be one, as You, Father, are in Me, and I in You; that they also may be one in Us, that the world may believe that You sent Me.(v.21)" - John 17:2

In John 17 we find the grand dream of Jesus for His Church. He would soon entrust His disciples with the mandate of the Great Commission, but now His prayer was for team unity to exist among this ragtag band of leaders. Jesus prayed that the Church would also experience the same unity found in the Godhead.

Christ's dream has never changed. He still has a dream that His Church would be a unified team filled with a love for God, which lays aside prejudice and personal agenda for the sake of the harvest. Only with a unified team will the world be won to Christ.

It is our passion that the **DREAM SUMMIT** on Saturday night and Sunday will be an opportunity for the local church to discover anew the prayer and passion of Jesus. Every church has a unique fingerprint, yet the key ingredients of a Biblical church will always include prayer, compassion outreach, soul-winning, and discipleship. It is our goal that over this weekend the local church will be mobilized to become the fulfillment of the dream Jesus has for His Church.

Preliminary Planning:

Dream Summit Weekend

CHECK-OFF LIST

I. HOW TO PREPARE FOR THE DREAM SUMMIT

The Strategic Plan: *DREAM SUMMIT WEEKEND*

The goal of the weekend is for the pastor to introduce the congregation to God's dream for their church and a strategic plan for implementation. A simple organization is put in place by the time the weekend is over, and people are recruited on Sunday morning to serve on one of four ministry teams.

Before the Saturday/Sunday DREAM SUMMIT weekend the pastor will:

1.__PREACH A SERMON SERIES INTRODUCING TEAM-UP EVANGELISM

2. __SELECT A DREAM TEAM
Recruit Four Team captains who have gifts and passions in four areas
__A TEAM: Advance Prayer Team Captain_____
__B TEAM: Bridge-Builders Team Captain_____
__C TEAM: Conversion Coaches Team Captain_____
__D TEAM: Discipleship Trainers Team Captain_____

3. __HAVE EACH CAPTAIN RECRUIT SOME PEOPLE WHO CAN HELP SERVE AS LEADERS
Each Team will meet and begin to gather ideas for implementation
__*A Team* will create a prayer list of non-believers
__*B Team* will plan how to connect with the community doing outreach
__*C Team* will learn a plan of salvation
__*D Team* will study the discipleship lessons together

4. __PREPARE INSTRUCTIONAL MATERIAL FOR

TRAINING THE TEAM LEADERS
5.___BRING TEAM CAPTAINS AND THEIR
LEADERS TOGETHER FOR INSTRUCTION
6. ___FORM A NEW AND RENEWING CHRISTIANS
CLASS/GROUP
___Equip teacher/leader to facilitate the class/group
___Enlist the newest believers in the church for a pilot
group

II. DREAM SUMMIT WEEKEND
Weekend Implementation:
Saturday Night Dream Summit: The evening will feature
a teaching time by the Pastor on the theme of *"God's Dream
for Your Church."* This teaching will help the leaders of
the church to envision what God's dreams might be for
their congregation. The church will discover anew *"Why
God placed us here as a church."* The final stage of the
evening will be to introduce *"God's Teams for Your Church"*
through the four biblical teams. The group will understand
how these four teams can help fulfill God's dreams for their
church, and vital ministry to their community.

Saturday 4:00– 8:45
___4:00 PM: Pastor & team captains meet for weekend
overview and prayer
___6:00 PM: Team captains and their teams gather for
light finger foods and fellowship
___6:30 PM: "God's Dream for Your Church"
PowerPoint presentation
___7:00 PM: Discussion followed by break
___7:30 PM: "God's Teams for Your Church"
PowerPoint presentation
___8:00 PM: Q & A followed by discussion in small
groups

_____8:30 PM: WRAP-UP: teams pray together

Sunday Worship

On Sunday morning the pastor will preach a special message about *"God's Dreams for His Church, How to Give our Church Away."* The sermon should ask three key questions of the congregation: *What is God's dream for this church?*, *What is keeping this church from reaching that dream?*, and *What are we celebrating?* The sermon could conclude with a recruitment of the congregation to serve on one of the four ministry teams. At the conclusion of the message, people will be asked to complete a commitment card to join one of the teams. To conclude the service, they will be asked to join their team leader in a designated place in the church for a team introduction and prayer together.

Following the message......
_____Each leader holds up sign with the name of a team
_____Invitation to prayerfully consider joining a team and sign card
_____Follow team leader to designated area for a five-minute team meeting and prayer

III. AFTER DREAM SUMMIT WEEKEND
_____Team captains meet and select names to call of all regular attendees who were absent for **THE DREAM SUMMIT WEEKEND** to give them an opportunity to participate.
_____Pastor meets with each team as soon as possible, to affirm strategy and offer encouragement
_____Pastor empowers team captains to lead their teams
_____Ongoing training and regular motivation sessions are provided

___Pastor continues mentoring/leadership development with team captains
___Victories are continually celebrated.
___Repeat process until Jesus comes

IV. TEAM-UP FOLLOW-THROUGH
___*A Team* prays for & gives names on prayer List to *B Team*
___*B Team* builds relationships & gives names to *C Team*
___*C Team* leads people to Christ & gives names to *D Team*
___*D Team* mentors new believers for 12 to 20 weeks

TEAM-UP WRAP-UP

THE GREAT COMMISSION MANDATE

"Therefore, go and make disciples of all the nations, baptizing them in the name of the Father and the Son and the Holy Spirit. Teach these new disciples to obey all the commands I have given you...."
-Matthew 28:19, 20

The Leadership: There is no dream without a team. And there is no team without the support and leadership of the senior pastor. To make Dreams to Teams successful it will take the pastor being 100% in support of the process and the end goal. This is not an event, but the initiation of a new phase of biblical effective ministry. Phone conversations between the pastor and team captains will need to be conducted regularly to answer questions. There may be a need for consultation on the details of the pre-weekend recruitment and training event. Before the weekend, there will need to be discernment and consultation in choosing the four key team members. The right people in the right places of leadership will provide the foundation for the successful team-building weekend.

*   **NOTE:** Where a small church is unable to find four key people to provide leadership to the four groups, the pastor could serve as leader of the soul-winning and discipleship group, and two other key leaders will be recruited in the area of prayer and outreach. In smaller churches, additional leaders may not be available. In that case, begin with just the team leader and add leaders as they become available.

TEACHING NOTES FOR THE DREAM SUMMIT

Part 1: GOD'S DREAM FOR YOUR CHURCH

A God-sized dream is the only foundation upon which to build a church.

Definition of a Spiritual Dreamer:
A person with a God-given capacity, and a God-given responsibility, who dreams a God-sized dream and is willing to be used by God to help bring God's dream to pass.

A GOD-SIZED DREAM IS...
1. *THE BIG PICTURE*
   A description of the future from God's perspective.
2. *THE GREAT MOTIVATOR*
   Specific enough to cause great excitement...even apprehension.
3. *OVERWHELMING*
   It unfolds and increases over time as God reveals more and more in response to our obedience.
4. *A SPIRITUAL FORCE*
   Carried and empowered by the wind and fire of the Holy Spirit. Nothing can withstand the strength of a God-sized dream!

Part 2: GOD'S TEAMS FOR YOUR CHURCH

A God-anointed team is the best way to reach a community for Christ.

THE ROAD TO EFFECTIVE EVANGELISM
1. **MOBLIZE THE WHOLE CHURCH** *to reach the community for Christ.*
2. **RECRUIT EVERY BELIEVER** *according to giftedness, calling, passion, and time availability.*
3. **DEVELOP FOUR TEAMS** *to do the work of evangelism.*

TEAM-UP EVANGELISM IS...
A <u>**STRATEGY:**</u> *to involve the whole church in the MISSION of evangelism.*
A <u>**STRUCTURE:**</u> *to include all the MEANS of evangelism.*
A <u>**SYNERGY:**</u> *to inspire the local church to MAXIMIZE its evangelism potential in new, creative, and practical ways!*

FOUR HARVEST TEAMS
A-**TEAM: ADVANCE PRAYERS WARRIORS,** *Praying Together for Results*
B-**TEAM: BRIDGE- BUILDERS,** *Building Relationships with Non-Believers*
C-**TEAM: CONVERSION COACHES,** *Helping People Pray to Receive Christ*
D-**TEAM: DISCIPLESHIP TRAINERS,** *Guiding People in Spiritual Formation*

RESOURCES

THE FIVE SERMONS PASTOR TOM PREACHED

Pastor Tom introduced the concept of the Team-UP

Evangelism to the congregation with five messages….

1st MESSAGE: GOD'S UNANSWERED QUESTION

The question before us: "Is anything too hard for the Lord?" -God, Genesis 18:14

Our immediate response is NO, yet our lifestyle response is MAYBE.

Most people around the world pray. They do so because they want God's help in tough times.

HOW DID ABRAHAM LEARN TO PRAY FOR OTHERS?
Abraham began to pray what was on the heart of God.
Sadly, most never consider how to pray what is on the heart of God.
It was not the prayer of judgment, but of mercy.

How Abraham Learned to Pray for Others...6 Observations

1. ABRAHAM'S PRAYER WAS A PERSONAL PRAYER
"Please stay awhile" –Genesis 18:5 (NLT)
Personal Intimacy WITH God Precedes Public Effectiveness FOR God
Many in Christian service rush to the doing part before they take care of the being part.

2. ABRAHAM'S PRAYER WAS A PETITION PRAYER
"Would you spare the city if there are only fifty good people in it? 18:24 (CEV)

3. ABRAHAM'S PRAYER WAS A PERCEPTIVE PRAYER
"Should not the judge of all the earth do right?"
Genesis 18:25b

4. ABRAHAM'S PRAYER WAS A PRESUMPTIOUS PRAYER
"I am nothing more than the dust of the earth. Please forgive me, Lord for daring to speak to you like this."
-Genesis 18:27 (CEV)
> *Humility Is Always a Prerequisite to Faith-Based Praying.*

5. ABRAHAM'S PRAYER WAS A PERSISTENT PRAYER
"Then Abraham pressed his request further." -Genesis 18:29 (NLT)
> *Never Take "NO" For an Answer When Praying for Souls*

6. ABRAHAM'S PRAYER WAS A PERSUASIVE PRAYER
"I will speak but once more! Suppose only ten are found there?" And the Lord said, "Then, for the sake of the ten, I will not destroy it." -18:32 (NLT)
> *Abraham Stopped Asking Before God Stopped Giving*

2ᴺᴰ MESSAGE: GETTING THE CHURCH
OUT OF THE CHURCH

There is a chasm that exists between the church and the culture around it.

There can never be a COME until first there has been a GO

LOOK AT HOW BARNABAS SPANNED THE GREAT DIVIDE BY BUILDING RELATIONSHIP BRIDGES.
Never underestimate the power of a bridge-building Barnabas!

Building bridges of compassion is the way to get the church out of the church.

1. BRIDGE-BUILDERS ARE ETERNALLY OPTIMISTIC
"Nicknamed Barnabas which means son of encouragement." 4:36

2. BRIDGE-BUILDERS GO BEYOND THE MINIMUM
"He sold a field he owned and brought the money to the apostles for those in need." -Acts 4:37
   a. They have a passion to serve others   Acts 4:34-35
   b. They have a spirit of generosity 4:37

3. BRIDGE-BUILDERS ARE ALWAYS REACHING OUT
   Here is Barnabas' List
         By giving money to people in need. 4:37
         By befriending an arch enemy of the church 9:27
         By meeting new people in other communities 11:22
         By bringing a rejected man back into ministry 11.25
         By bringing gifts to believers in need 11:30
         By going abroad as a missionary 13:1-3
         By witnessing to the governor 13:7
         By encouraging many to remain faithful 13:43
         By forcing early church to modify rules for new converts 15
         By befriending ministry dropouts 15:39

4. BRIDGE-BUILDERS TAKE CALCULATED RISKS

"Then Barnabas brought Saul to the apostles." -Acts 9:26
   a. They accept the unacceptable
   b. They put others ahead of themselves

5. BRIDGEBUILDERS ARE MISSION FOCUSED

"The Church sent Barnabas to Antioch." -Acts 11:22
   a. They are always ready for new opportunities. Acts 11:22
   b. They understand what God blesses. Acts 11:23

6. BRIDGEBUILDERS ARE SPIRIT-FILLED

"Barnabas was a good man, full of the Holy Spirit." -Acts 11:24
   a. They are only effective when Spirit-led
   b. They give all the glory to God

7. BRIDGEBUILDERS GET THE JOB DONE

"And large numbers of people were brought to the Lord." 11:24
   a. They know the main thing is to bring people to Christ
   b. They are the pacesetters of church growth

"It was there at Antioch that the believers were first called Christians." -Acts 11:26

There is a greater chasm than the one that exists between the church and her world.
It is the chasm that Christ bridged on the cross that exists between a holy God and a sinful man.

3rd MESSAGE: OUT OF THEIR FACES AND INTO THEIR SHOES

"Live wisely among those who are not Christians, and make the most of every opportunity. Let your conversation be gracious and effective so that you will have the right answer for everyone." -Colossians 4:5-6

Andrew never preached like Peter or wrote like Paul. He never held office like James, nor was a creative thinker like John. He didn't make the elite inner circle. He was an ordinary businessman who fished out of a small boat on the Sea of Galilee. Never made the headlines, most often inconspicuous in what he did. Didn't speak to the masses, but to the individuals. But Andrew was the first called Apostle of Jesus Christ, a caller of others before he was called himself. Andrew was frequently called Protokletos, first called. First to come to Christ, first home missionary, first foreign missionary. Andrew's life could be summed up with this sentence:

TO KNOW CHRIST AND TO MAKE HIM KNOWN!
Andrew is known primarily as the One who Brought Others to Jesus. How Andrew Brought Others to Christ....

1. ANDREW CHOSE TO BE A FIRST RESPONDER
"Then John's two disciples turned and followed Jesus" –John 1:37
   a. First responders are gripped with a sense of urgency
   b. First responders keep focused on mission

2. ANDREW ASKED POWERFUL QUESTIONS
"Where are you staying?" - John 1:38

   a. Insightful questions pave the way for honest answers
   b. Learn more by listening than by talking

3. ANDREW PURSUED PERSONAL PREPARATION
"It was about four o'clock in the afternoon when they went with him to the place, and they stayed there the rest of the day." -John 1:39
   a. Nurtured a personal relationship
   b. Gained a wealth of knowledge

4. ANDREW PERSUADED WITH PASSION

"The first thing Andrew did was to find his brother Simon." John 1:41
   a. What he found he wanted everyone else to find
   b. Live so your witness is most effective to those who are closest to you

5. ANDREW ANSWERED THE CALL

"Come, be my disciples, and I will show you how to fish for people! And they left their nets at once and went with him." –Matthew 4:19
   a. To some, a call to be out front, to others it is a call to work behind the scenes
   b. To all it is a call to fish for people!

6. ANDREW PROBLEM-SOLVED KINGDOM-BUILDING

"Then Andrew, Simon Peter's brother, spoke up. There's a young boy here." –John 6:8-9
   a. Every prospect has hidden resources to help build the kingdom
   b. Bringing people to Jesus solves the problem of Kingdom deficiency

7. ANDREW BROUGHT "WHOSOEVER WILL" TO CHRIST

"(Some Greeks) They approached Philip: 'Sir, we want to see Jesus. Can you help us?' Philip went and told Andrew." -John 12:20-22
   a. Andrew lived to be a coach and a guide. I like to call Andrew a DESTINY COACH.
   b. Andrew knew no boundaries or limitations to reaching others

4ᵀᴴ MESSAGE: GO AND MAKE DISCIPLES

"Hold on to the pattern of right teaching you learned from me. And remember to live in the faith and love that you have in Christ Jesus. With the help of the Holy Spirit who lives within us, carefully guard what has been entrusted to you. –II Timothy 1:13-14 (NLT)

How Timothy Made and Multiplied Disciples

We first catch a glimpse of Timothy in Acts 16:1 where Paul found him as a young disciple in Lystra. Paul saw great potential in this timid young man so he invited him to go with him. Most disciple-makers choose their disciples. Jesus modeled that, as did Paul.

"Timothy, my son, here are my instructions for you." I Timothy 1:18

What Made Timothy a Great Disciple-Maker?
1. THE PURPOSE OF DISCIPLE-MAKING
"The purpose of my instruction is that all the Christians there would be filled with love that comes from a pure heart, a clear conscience, and a sincere faith." - I Timothy 1:5
At the very heart of the discipleship process is the concept of modeling
WE WILL HAVE BETTER CHRISTIANS WHEN WE HAVE BETTER DISCIPLE-MAKERS

2. THE PREPARATION OF A DISCIPLE-MAKER
"You have the faith of your mother, Eunice, and your grandmother" - 2ⁿᵈ Timothy 1:5   What was Paul saying?
  To Be a Mentor, One Must First Be Mentored. To Give, you must have received something so you can give!
  Disciple-Makers Are First Discipled Themselves so They Can Become Disciplers and Disciple-Makers of Others

3. THE POWER OF A DISCIPLE-MAKER
"Fan into flames the spiritual gift God gave you." 2ⁿᵈ Timothy 1:6
  Fire burns only as long as it has fuel
    Disciple-Makers Keep a Passionate Heart Hot for God

4. THE PROCESS OF DISCIPLE-MAKING

"You have heard me teach many things...teach these great truths to trustworthy people who are able to pass them on to others." 2nd *Timothy 2:2*

Definition of Discipleship: Equipping believers to multiply themselves through the mentoring of others.

DISCIPLE-MAKING IS A MULTIPLICATION PROCESS

LEVEL 1: Of course it begins with Jesus Christ, the Master Disciple-Maker

LEVEL 2: Saul turned Paul, who learned from Christ

LEVEL 3: Timothy who learned from Paul

LEVEL 4: Faithful & trustworthy disciples who learned from Timothy

LEVEL 5: More faithful and trustworthy disciples who learned from faithful and trustworthy disciples

....And the list goes on....

.

5. THE PICTURE OF A DISCIPLE-MAKER   (II Timothy 2)

A disciple-maker is expressed in at least four ways.

A Teacher: Known by complete devotion to <u>Life Change</u>. (verse 2)

Key Characteristic: Reproduction

A Soldier: Known by complete devotion to <u>Endurance</u>. (verse 3)

Key Characteristic: Focus

An Athlete: Known by complete devotion to the <u>Goal.</u> (verse 5)

Key Characteristic: Competence

A Farmer: Known by complete devotion to the <u>Process</u>. (verse 6)

Key characteristic: Hard Work

5<u>TH</u> MESSAGE: HOW TO GIVE OUR CHURCH AWAY

Three Parables from Luke 15.

church with a little <u>"c"</u> is a building in the neighborhood.

Church with a big <u>"C"</u> is the people of God invading the neighborhood.

The way we view lost people reveals our true heart for God!

People who don't attend our church need it more than the people who do attend.

I. THE SHEPHERD AND HIS ONE LOST SHEEP

Shall I Stay or Go?

II. THE WOMAN AND HER ONE LOST SILVER COIN

Shall I Sit or Search?

III. THE FATHER AND HIS LOST SON

Shall I Reject or Reinstate?

There are two kinds of churches who have two different ways of looking at lost people

Loving father churches and older brother churches

In the story of the Lost Son we find the two kinds of churches Jesus taught about

Jesus taught there are only two ways to look at the Lost Son/only two ways to treat him

With the warm heart of the Loving Father

With the cold heart of the Older Brother

Loving Father was preoccupied with the son who was missing—all about him

Older Brother was preoccupied with the son who stayed home—all about me

Loving Father had the spirit of compassion with the offer of forgiveness

Older Brother had the spirit of condemnation with the offer of shame

Loving Father confronted Older Brother thinking

Older Brother criticized Loving Father thinking

Loving Father keeps the lights on and the door open

Older Brother closes the door and turns out the lights

Loving Father threw parties

Older Brother threw fits

What would have happened that day if instead of the Loving Father coming out on the porch and looking up the road when the prodigal son was coming, it had been the older brother?

> There would have been no pounding heart of love
>
> No run to meet him
>
> No warm embrace
>
> No forgiveness

 208

No fatted calf killed

No welcome home party

How does our church treat the prodigal when they visit our church?

    As the Older Brother?

    As the Loving Father?

Can we become a Loving Father Church?

Ignite a new fire for Evangelism by moving from Dreams to Teams
A. TEAM-Advance Prayer Warriors who pray together for results
B. TEAM-Bridge-Builders who build bridges of friendship and compassion
C. TEAM-Conversion Coaches who help people come to saving faith
D. TEAM-Discipleship Trainers who guide people in spiritual formation

Three steps we all need to take to give our church away:
1. Fall in love with Jesus afresh and anew
2. Ask God to show us the "MORE" we should give/do
3. Begin where we are with what we have to bring MORE Glory to God

TOGETHER WE BURN BRIGHTER

Helping Churches Make the GRADE.....
WITH THE TEAM-UP TRAINING SYSTEM

Life change evangelism is a practical evangelism system designed to assist local churches reach their communities for Christ.

The Team –UP Harvesting Cycle Consists Of:
1. **PREPARING THE SOIL**
   THE PRAYER WARRIORS: Abraham
2. **PLANTING THE SEED**
   THE BRIDGE-BUILDERS: Barnabas
3. **PICKING THE CROP**
   THE SOUL-WINNERS: Andrew
4. **PROTECTING THE CROP**
   THE DISCIPLE-MAKERS: Timothy

FOUR GROUPS MAKE UP THE TEAM-UP SYSTEM
1. THE PRAYER WARRIERS: ABRAHAM
   Prayer Partners
   Prayer Cells
   Prayer Corps
   Prayer Chain
   Prayer Vigil
   Prayer and Fasting
2. THE BRIDGE BUILDERS: BARNABAS
   Neighborhood Connections
   Acts of Kindness
   Servant Projects
   Social Events
   Visitation Teams

Hospital
New Move-Ins
Needs Survey
3. THE SOUL-WINNERS: ANDREW
The Gospel Presentation
4. THE DISCIPLE-MAKERS: TIMOTHY
Bible Study options for New and Renewing Christians

Individual Bible Study: Personal Bible Study (3

Lessons) (Formerly Timothy Lessons)
Group Bible Study: New Life Adventure
(Formerly New Converts Lessons)

(Part 1, 7 Lessons)

(Part 2, 7 Lessons)

One-to-One Discipleship: Timothy Lessons (10

Lessons)

AVAILABLE RESOURCES FOR MAKING DISCIPLES
LEADERSHIP DEVELOPMENT FOR TEAM CAPTAINS

Building Teams in Ministry by Dale Galloway
Beacon Hill Press, 2000
Pulling Together, The Power of Teamwork by John J. Murphy
Wynwood, 1997
Team Spirit, (a management handbook) by David Cormack
Zondervan, 1989
Doing Church as a Team by Wayne Cordeiro
Regal, 2001
Teach your Team to Fish by Laurie Beth Jones
Crown Business, 2002
The Coach Approach to Evangelism and Discipleship
On Purpose Ministries and The Wesleyan Church, 2005

A TEAM: PRAYER WARRIORS-Praying Together for Results

Touch the World Through Prayer by Wesley L. Duewel
Francis Asbury Press, 1986

P.R.A.Y.E.R. a Priority of the Church by Thomas D. Kinnan

B TEAM: BRIDGE BUILDERS—Reaching Out to Others
Compassion Evangelism by Thomas G. Nees
Beacon Hill Press, 1996
The Church of Irresistible Influence by Robert Lewis
Zondervan, 2001
101 Ways to Reach Your Community by Steve Sjogren
Navpress, 2001
101 Ways to Help People in Need by Steve and Janie Sjogren
Navpresss, 2002
Conspiracy of Kindness by Steve Sjogren
Regal, 2003
Like your Neighbor by Stephen W. Sorenson
Intervarsity Press, 2005
Finding Common Ground by Tim Downs
Moody Press, 1999
The Connecting Church by Randy Frazee
Zondervan, 2001
Making Room for Life by Randy Frazee
Zondervan, 2003
Dog Training, Fly Fishing, & Sharing Christ by Ted Haggard
Thomas Nelson, 2002
Concentric Circles of Concern by W. Oscar Thompson
Broadman & Holman, 1999

A program called "Acts of Random Kindness," or "A.R.K." has been developed for churches: a practical, structured "good deeds" program that helps congregations mobilize and organize their members to offer tangible acts of help within their communities. *For details: www.arkalmighty.com.*

C TEAM: CONVERSION COACHES--Helping People Come to Faith

Irresistible Evangelism by Sjogren, Ping, and Pollock
  Group, 2004
Questioning Evangelism by Randy Newman
  Kregel, 2004
Going Public with Your Faith, William Carr Peel & Walt Larimore
  Zondervan, 2003
Mission to OZ by Mark Tabb
  Moody, 2004
Permission Evangelism By Michael L Simpson
  Nexgen, 2003
Can We Talk by Robert G. Tuttle, Jr
  Abingdon Press, 1999
Out of Their Faces and Into Their Shoes by John Kramp
  Broadman & Holman Publishers, 1995
One to One by Michael Green
  Moorings, 1995
Becoming a Contagious Christian by Bill Hybels & Mark Mittelberg
  Zondervan, 1994
Evangelism Outside the Box by Rick Richardson
  InterVarsity Press, 2000
Inside the Mind of Unchurched Harry & Mary by Lee Strobel
  Zondervan, 1993
Life-Style Evangelism by Joseph C. Aldrich
  Multnomah Press, 1981
Evangelism as a Lifestyle by Jim Petersen
  Navpress, 1980
The Unchurched Next Door by Thom S. Rainer
  Zondervan, 2003

D TEAM: DISCIPLESHIP TRAINERS
Guiding People in Spiritual Formation

Individual Bible Study: Personal Bible Study Book (Three Lessons)
Group Bible Study: New Life Adventure Books I & II (Fourteen Lessons)
One to One Discipleship: Timothy Lessons (Ten Lessons)
The Alpha Course by Nicky Gumbel

Disciples are Made Not Born by Walter A. Henrichsen
Victor Books, 1988
The Lost Art of Disciple Making by Leroy Eims
Zondervan Publishing House, 1978
The Disciple Making Pastor by Bill Hull
Fleming H. Revel, 1988
Jesus Christ Disciple Maker by Bill Hull
Fleming H. Revel, 1990
With Christ in the School of Disciple Building by Carl Wilson
Zondervan, 1976
Side by Side, Disciple-Making for a New Century by General Editors
Cook & Navpress, 2000

These are only a few of the resources that are available today. Your local bookstore can help you with many more just for the asking.

READING LIST

In His Steps by Charles M. Sheldon, Chicago Advance Publishing Co. 1896

The Sky Pilot by Ralph Connor, Grosset and Dunlap, 1899

The Victories of Wesley Castle by C. W. Winchester, The Christian Witness Co. 1900

The Calling of Dan Matthews by Harold Bell Wright, A. L. Burt Company, 1909

The Revival Secret by H. Robb French, Wesleyan Methodist Publishing House, 1934

Martinko by Kristina Roy, Bible Light Publishers, Date Unknown

Evangelism That Works by George Barna, Regal Books, 1995

Compassion Evangelism by Thomas G. Nees, Beacon Hill Press, 1996

Friends: How to Evangelize Generation X by Ralph Moore, Straight Street Publishing, 1997

Finding Common Ground by Tim Downs, Moody Press, 1999

Evangelism Outside the Box by Rick Richardson, Intervarsity Press, 2000

101 Ways to Reach Your Community by Steve Sjogren, Navpress, 2001

101 Ways to Help People in Need by Steve and Jamie Sjogren, Navpress, 2002

Sharing Your Life Mission Every Day by Eastman, Wendorff & Thorp, Zondervan, 2002

Permission Evangelism by Michael L. Simpson, Nexgen, 2003

Conspiracy of Kindness by Steve Sjogren, Regal, 2003

Going Public with Your Faith by William Carr Peel & Walt Larimore, Zondervan, 2003

Mission to OZ by Mark Tabb, Moody Publishers, 2004

Irresistible Evangelism by Steve Sjogren, Dave Ping & Doug Polock, Group, 2004

Questioning Evangelism by Randy Newman, Kregal, 2004

X-Factor Evangelism by Michael Wiles, ChurchSmart Resources, 2005

Like Your Neighbor? By Stephen W. Sorenson, Intervarsity Press, 2005

CPSIA information can be obtained at www.ICGtesting.com
Printed in the USA
LVOW02s1215080714

392992LV00003B/6/P